# Intersexuality and the Law

# Intersexuality and the Law

*Why Sex Matters*

Julie A. Greenberg

NEW YORK UNIVERSITY PRESS
*New York and London*

NEW YORK UNIVERSITY PRESS
New York and London
www.nyupress.org

References to Internet websites (URLs) were accurate at the time of writing.
Neither the author nor New York University Press is responsible for URLs
that may have expired or changed since the manuscript was prepared.

Library of Congress Cataloging-in-Publication Data

Greenberg, Julie A.
Intersexuality and the law : why sex matters / Julie A. Greenberg.
p. cm.
Includes bibliographical references and index.
ISBN 978-0-8147-3189-5 (cl : alk. paper)
ISBN 978-0-8147-3860-3 (ebook)
ISBN 978-0-8147-3861-0 (ebook)
1. Intersex people—Legal status, laws, etc.—United States. 2. Intersex people—United
States—Social conditions. I. Title.
KF478.5.G74      2011
346.7301'3—dc23          2011028193

New York University Press books are printed on acid-free paper,
and their binding materials are chosen for strength and durability.
We strive to use environmentally responsible suppliers and materials
to the greatest extent possible in publishing our books.

Manufactured in the United States of America

10 9 8 7 6 5 4 3 2 1

*To my family, Rob, Danny, and Sean Irving,*
*for their love and support.*

*To the many people with an intersex condition whose dignity*
*and dedication to improving the lives of people who confront*
*these issues on a daily basis inspired this project.*

# Contents

# Acknowledgments

I am grateful to so many people whose work, support, and inspiration made this book possible. Sherri Groveman Morris is responsible for introducing me to and patiently educating me about intersexuality and the critical issues confronting people with an intersex condition. Bo Laurent sensitized me to the complex medical and ethical issues surrounding the treatment of infants with an intersex condition. My fellow members on the board of Advocates for Informed Choice and especially its executive director, Anne Tamar-Mattis, furthered my knowledge and critical thinking about the topics discussed in this book.

The faculty, staff, and students at Thomas Jefferson School of Law provided invaluable support for this project. The school financially supported this work with summer stipends, a sabbatical, and research assistant support. Lively conversations with the faculty and students in my "Women and the Law" and "Sexuality, Gender and the Law" courses helped to shape my ideas as they developed. Law school librarians Karla Castetter, Patrick Meyer, June MacLeod, Dorothy Hampton, Hadas Livant, Jane Larrington, Leigh Inman, and Catherine Deane miraculously found difficult-to-attain international, medical, psychological, and historical sources. Faculty assistant Randy Ward provided patient and efficient support through my more intense emotional moments and faculty assistant Skylar Rzyhill contributed her stellar proofreading skills. Student research assistants Erin Goldie, Anne Knight, Vera Valdivia, Nick Cassidy, Chris Dailey, and Joe Visic spent countless hours researching, proofreading, and cite checking.

A number of people provided extraordinarily helpful comments on manuscript drafts. Nancy Ehrenreich, Ellen Feder, Miriam Frank, Marybeth Herald, Linda Keller, David Knight, Anne Tamar-Mattis, David Meyer, and Catherine Thiemann provided extensive suggestions that assisted me in fine-tuning my thinking on a number of critical issues and vastly improved the manuscript.

I am also grateful to the faculty, students, and staff at the Research Centre for Law, Gender and Sexuality at Keele University and Kent University. During my time as a visiting scholar with the Centre during the early stages of writing this book, I had the opportunity to engage in critical conversations with a number of people that enormously assisted in shaping the final project. I also benefited from discussions at faculty forums sponsored by the Williams Institute at the University of California–Los Angeles and Hofstra University Law School.

I am indebted to the editors at NYU Press for their thoughtful and thorough comments on the manuscript. I want to especially acknowledge Deborah Gershenowitz for her encouragement in the early stages of this project.

Most important, I am grateful to my spouse, Rob Irving, whose love, understanding, and extraordinary editorial skills helped bring this book to fruition.

# Introduction

Media interest in intersexuality has blossomed over the past decade. Stories about people with an intersex condition have been the focus of dozens of books, movies, television dramas, and documentaries. Similarly, in academia, intersexuality has moved from being a relatively obscure topic, examined in a handful of medical journals, to becoming the central topic of numerous books and articles in a variety of disciplines, including psychology, history, anthropology, and medical ethics.

Intersexuality has also become a hot topic in legal circles. In the past ten years, more than a hundred legal articles and books have included a discussion of intersexuality. Most of these publications do not focus on the issues that have a direct effect on the lives of people with an intersex condition. Instead, most of these publications have used the existence of intersexuality to support the expansion of rights of other sexual minorities, including members of the lesbian, gay, bisexual, and transsexual (LGBT) communities.

Understanding how the issues that are critical to people with an intersex condition can be conflated with the issues affecting other people who challenge sex and gender norms requires a basic understanding of the nature of intersexuality. The meaning of the term *intersex* has varied and the issue is still a topic of sometimes heated discussion.[1] Although doctors and activists in the intersex community continue to debate exactly what conditions qualify as "intersex," I am using the term in its broadest sense to include anyone with a congenital condition whose sex chromosomes, gonads, or internal or external sexual anatomy do not fit clearly into the binary male/female norm. Some intersex conditions involve an inconsistency between a person's internal and external sexual features. For example, some people with an intersex condition may have female appearing external genitalia, no internal female organs, and testicles. Other people with an intersex condition may be born with genitalia that do not appear to be clearly male or female. For example, a girl may be born with a larger than average clitoris and no vagina. Similarly, a boy may be born with a small penis and a divided scrotum that resembles labia. Some people with an intersex condition may also be born with a chromosomal pattern that does not fall into the binary XX/XY norm.

Not all intersex conditions are apparent at the time of birth; some conditions are not evident until a child reaches puberty and fails to develop typical male or female traits. For example, the condition may be discovered when a girl reaches puberty and fails to menstruate.

Because experts do not agree on exactly which conditions fit within the definition of intersexuality and some conditions are not evident until years after a child is born, it is impossible to state with precision exactly how many people have an intersex condition. Most experts agree that approximately 1–2 percent of people are born with sexual features that vary from the medically defined norm for male and female. Approximately one in fifteen hundred to one in two thousand births involve a child who is born with genitalia so noticeably atypical that a specialist in sex differentiation is consulted and surgical alteration is considered.[2]

Some people are confused about how intersexuality compares to transsexuality and transgenderism. The meaning of these latter two terms also varies. The term *transsexual* is commonly used to refer to a person who does not have an intersex condition whose gender self-identity does not match the sex assigned at birth. The term includes preoperative, postoperative, and nonoperative transsexuals. Many people use the word *transgender* as an umbrella term that encompasses anyone who transgresses sex or gender boundaries. The term *transgender* may include transsexuals, transvestites, or others whose dress or behavior fails to conform to gender norms.

Society and legal institutions frequently confuse intersexuality and transsexuality and inappropriately conflate the discrete concepts of sex, sexual orientation, gender presentation/gender role,[3] and gender identity. Table 1 illustrates prevailing societal presumptions about men and woman and the groups that directly challenge those assumptions.

Society presumes that men display the attributes in the first column and women display the characteristics in the second column. In other words, men are presumed to have male anatomy, to be sexually attracted to females, to appear masculine and fulfill male roles, and to self-identify as men. Women are presumed to have female anatomy, to be sexually attracted to men, to be caregiving and feminine, and to self-identify as women. These presumptions are not true for millions of people and they are being challenged by people with an intersex condition, gays, lesbians, bisexuals, feminists, men and women who do not conform to gender stereotypes, and transsexuals.

**TABLE 1**

*Assumptions about Males and Females and
the People Who Challenge Those Assumptions*

| | Males: assumptions | Females: assumptions | Challengers |
|---|---|---|---|
| *Sexual/ reproductive anatomy* | penis, scrotum, testicles, XY chromosomes | clitoris, labia, vagina, uterus, fallopian tubes, XX chromosomes | People with an intersex condition |
| *Sexual orientation* | Toward women | Toward men | Gays, lesbians, and bisexuals |
| *Gender presentation/ gender role* | Masculine | Feminine | Feminists and men and women who fail to conform to gender stereotypes |
| *Gender identity* | Male | Female | Transsexuals |

The existence of people with an intersex condition whose bodies combine aspects of male and female anatomy provides a perfect rhetorical device for challenging traditional notions of sex, gender, and sexual orientation. Because intersex bodies fail to fit neatly into the traditional male/female binary construct, intersexuality can be used to call into question our basic notions of what it means to be a man or a woman.

If we cannot easily establish what makes a man a man or a woman a woman, feminists can assert that the rationale for any sex based distinctions is seriously undermined. Furthermore, if society cannot straightforwardly differentiate men from women, then gays, lesbians, and bisexuals can argue that same-sex relationships cannot be legitimately condemned. Finally, if gender identity does not necessarily develop in concert with sexual anatomy, as recent studies of children with an intersex condition indicate, then transsexuals' claims for legal recognition of their self-identified gender are bolstered. In other words, the existence of people with an intersex condition can be used to advance equality claims by feminists, gays, lesbians, bisexuals, and transsexuals. When other groups use the existence of intersexuality to bolster their claims, they sometimes fail to consider the effects that these arguments will have on members of the intersex community.

Activists working to enhance the rights of people with an intersex condition and advocates working on behalf of other sexual minorities, especially transsexual activists, share the common goal of eliminating harmful practices based on sex and gender stereotypes. In addition, both groups seek to enhance the right to sexual self-determination. The primary focus of each group differs, however.

The primary goal of the intersex movement is to eliminate or decrease the number of medically unnecessary cosmetic genital surgeries being performed on infants with an intersex condition. Intersex advocates believe that these medical interventions often result in physical and emotional trauma. They argue that no evidence exists that these surgeries are beneficial. Thus, they believe that these surgeries should not be performed on children and should only be undertaken with the informed consent of patients when they reach an age at which they can fully understand the risks and benefits and can decide for themselves whether they want to undergo cosmetic genital surgery.

The primary focus of the transsexual movement is to eliminate discriminatory practices that deny transsexuals the right to be treated as their self-identified sex. Although transsexual activists disagree about whether the ultimate goal should be eliminating entirely the gender binary norm or allowing transsexuals to freely cross the gender divide, transsexual activism has developed as an identity movement. Transsexual activists have aligned themselves closely with gay and lesbian organizations. They believe that the nature of the discrimination they suffer stems from the same animus directed against gays and lesbians. Their goal is to end discriminatory practices against people whose gender behavior and sexual practices do not conform to societal norms.

The intersex activist movement is still in its infancy and is in the process of developing its advocacy strategies. Some people in the intersex movement feel closely allied to LGBT activist groups. They believe that the societal and legal issues facing people with an intersex condition are similar to the issues confronting other sex and gender nonconformists. In addition, they think of "intersex" as an identity, similar to gay, lesbian, and transsexual identities. They believe that joining forces with LGBT organizations will assist people with an intersex condition in two ways. First, LGBT groups can offer the emotional support that a group identity movement can provide. In addition, some intersex activists view the legal issues facing LGBT people and people with an intersex condition as closely related and believe that working with the larger, well established LGBT organizations will help enhance the rights of people with an intersex condition.

Others in the intersex community do not feel closely allied with the LGBT movement. They believe that the primary harm threatening people with an intersex condition is the medical practice of surgically altering infants and cloaking the treatment in shame and secrecy. They recognize that the current medical protocol is based on stereotyped gender assumptions and heteronormativity. They believe, however, that altering the current medical protocol for the treatment of infants with an intersex condition can best be advanced by focusing on issues emphasized by disability rights advocates, including the right to autonomy and bodily integrity. These intersex advocates believe that the legal issues confronting people with an intersex condition are distinct from the primary focus of the LGBT movement and that forming alliances with LGBT groups may actually hinder their goal of ending surgeries on infants with an intersex condition. Some of these activists believe that adopting the strategies of the critical disability movement will be a more effective tool to protect people with an intersex condition.

Although scholars in a variety of disciplines, including medical ethics, history, psychology, sociology, and anthropology, have published books on intersexuality, none has examined the role that the law can play in enhancing the lives of people with an intersex condition. This book fills that gap. It explores the potential effectiveness of using legal challenges to accomplish the intersex movement's goals. It discusses the legal frameworks used by other social justice movements that have effectively brought challenges to discriminatory practices and explores whether the intersex movement can form mutually beneficial alliances with these other movements and use similar legal strategies.

Part I focuses on the medical practices that attempt to eliminate evidence of intersexuality by surgically altering infants so that they conform or blend into a medically created definition of normal genitalia. Chapter 1 explains the sex, gender, and disability assumptions underlying the current medical protocol. Although most intersex conditions are not disabling, pose no physical risk, and require no medical intervention, infants with an intersex condition are often subjected to invasive cosmetic surgeries to alter their genitalia so that their bodies conform to a binary sex norm.[4] For example, female infants who are born with a clitoris that is considered too large are frequently subjected to clitoral reduction surgery. Similar interventions are undertaken on males whose penises appear atypical. These surgeries provide no medical benefit and have not been proven to enhance the child's psychological well-being, but they often lead to a number of problems. These surgeries may render women incapable of experiencing an orgasm. They may also result in infection, scarring, incontinence, and other severe physical complications. Many medical experts, scholars, and people who have been subjected to these surgeries assert that these medical procedures often cause stigma, psychological trauma, and lifelong physical complications, without proof of any benefit to the child. They have advocated in favor of a moratorium on these medically unnecessary cosmetic surgeries.

Chapter 2 examines the legal approaches that could be adopted to successfully challenge these medical practices. It analyzes whether parents, in consultation with doctors, should have the legal power to consent to genital modification surgery on behalf of their children with an intersex condition. The Constitutional Court of Colombia, the only high court to address this issue, has placed severe restrictions on parents' ability to consent to cosmetic genital surgery because of concerns that parents may be discriminating against their own children. This chapter discusses the potential for courts in the United States and other countries to adopt a similar approach to ensure that the child's constitutional rights are adequately protected.

Part II of this book explores the areas in which the concerns of people with an intersex condition and the concerns of transsexuals may converge. It examines the state's role in determining a person's legal sex for those people who do not conform to sex and gender stereotypes. If the intersex movement succeeds in stopping medically unnecessary cosmetic surgeries, adults with an intersex condition may face the same legal obstacles that currently confront transsexuals. Chapter 3 provides an overview to the subjects discussed in this part.

Chapter 4 examines the most litigated area related to sex determination: establishing a person's sex for purposes of marriage. Recent court decisions have adopted diverse and contradictory approaches. Some states make this determination by relying on biological factors present at birth, including chromosomes, genitalia, and the ability to beget or bear children. Courts in these states typically find that a person's legal sex is permanently established at birth. Other states focus on the sex indicators that exist at the time a person seeks to marry and place a greater emphasis on the gender role in which the person is living. These states typically rule that legal sex may be different from the sex assigned at birth. Therefore, the legal sex of a person with an intersex condition or a transsexual may vary depending on the state in which the issue is litigated. Chapter 4 discusses these contradictory rulings that could potentially lead to the anomalous result that a person with an intersex condition or a transsexual could legally marry a man in some states, legally marry a woman in other states, and potentially be barred from marrying at all under some state definitions of male and female.

Chapter 5 discusses identity documents and analyzes whether people with an intersex condition and transsexuals should be allowed to create their own legal identity through the use of the name and sex indicator they choose on their official documents. As in the other areas discussed in this section of the book, courts and legislatures have adopted a kaleidoscope of approaches. Most states allow birth records and other identity documents to be amended so that the name and sex indicator correspond to the person's gender self-identity. In contrast, some states do not allow identity documents to be modified to reflect a sex or name change. In addition, the federal government has adopted rules for federal documents that vary from the rules adopted in the states. Thus, people may have some of their official documents indicate that they are male, while other documents indicate that they are female. This chapter examines the different viewpoints that have led to these contradictory outcomes.

Chapter 6 discusses sex classification for purposes of determining appropriate housing and restroom use. Courts have been asked to determine the sex of a person with an intersex condition or a transsexual for the purpose of establishing appropriate housing in prisons and bathroom use in public facilities. In making such determinations, courts have considered the privacy interests and safety concerns of the other people sharing the facility. This chapter explores these issues and analyzes whether society's sense of propriety and morality should be used to determine another person's right to sexual self-determination.

Part III explores how the intersex movement can most effectively frame legal arguments and build alliances with other progressive social justice movements to help advance its goals. Chapter 7 introduces the issues discussed in this part. Chapter 8 discusses the birth of the intersex movement and the development of its goals and strategies. Chapters 9 and 10 explore whether the intersex movement could advance its goals by developing legal arguments in conjunction with other social justice movements. Chapter 9 sets the stage by providing a history of the development of social justice movements that focus on discrimination based on sex, gender, sexual orientation, gender identity, and disability. It examines the problems that have arisen among the feminist, gay/lesbian/bisexual, transsexual, and intersex movements. Chapter 10 builds on chapter 9 by examining the legal arguments that other social justice movements have developed and discusses whether the intersex movement could effectively use similar approaches. The book concludes by discussing the benefits of forming mutually beneficial alliances with other movements challenging similar discriminatory actions.

The intersex movement is at a critical crossroads in its development. It could align itself with and frame its legal arguments in terms similar to those used by organizations fighting for sex and gender equality, it could adopt a critical disability framework and focus on the right to bodily autonomy, or it could adopt some combination of the two approaches. The goal of this book is to help shed light on which legal strategies may most effectively end discriminatory practices against people with an intersex condition and potentially assist other marginalized groups.

# PART I

## Gender Blending

# 1

# Surgical and Hormonal
# Creation of the Binary Sex Model

One of the few fundamental aspects of life is that of sex. . . . To visualize individuals who properly belong neither to one sex nor to the other is to imagine freaks, misfits, curiosities, rejected by society and condemned to a solitary existence of neglect and frustration. . . . The tragedy of their lives is the greater since it may be remediable; with suitable management and treatment, especially if this is begun soon after birth, many of these people can be helped to live happy well adjusted lives.[1]

This passage came from a 1960s medical text written by two respected doctors. The sentiments expressed in this book reflect the basis for the standard treatment protocol for infants born with an intersex condition, which began during the 1950s. This chapter examines the development of the dominant treatment protocol for infants with an intersex condition that began in the middle of the twentieth century and remained largely unchanged for fifty years. It examines the unproven assumptions about sex, gender, and disability that have shaped medical practices and describes the recent challenges that call these common practices into question.

## Sex Differentiation

Medical experts now recognize that at least eight attributes contribute to a person's sex. These factors include genetic or chromosomal sex, gonadal sex (reproductive sex glands), internal morphologic sex (seminal vesicles, prostate, vagina, uterus, and fallopian tubes), external morphologic sex (genitalia), hormonal sex (androgens or estrogens), phenotypic sex (secondary sexual features such as facial hair or breasts), assigned sex and gender of rearing, and gender identity.[2]

### The Typical Sex Differentiation Path

During the first seven weeks after conception, all human embryos are sexually undifferentiated. At seven weeks, the embryonic reproductive system consists of a pair of gonads that can grow into either ovaries (female) or testes (male). The genital ridge that exists at this point can develop into either a clitoris and labia (female) or a penis and scrotum (male). Two primordial duct systems also exist at this stage. The female ducts are called Mullerian ducts and develop into the uterus, fallopian tubes, and upper part of the vagina if the fetus follows the female path. The male ducts are called Wolffian ducts and are the precursors of the seminal vesicles, vas deferens, and epididymis.

At eight weeks, the fetus typically begins to follow one sex path. If the fetus has one X and one Y chromosome (46XY), it will start down the male path. At eight weeks, a switch on the Y chromosome, called the testis determining factor, signals the embryonic gonads to form into testes. The testes begin to produce male hormones. These male hormones prompt the genitals to develop male features. Additionally the testes produce a substance called Mullerian inhibiting factor that causes the female Mullerian ducts to atrophy and to be absorbed by the body, so that a female reproductive system is not created.

If the fetus has two X chromosomes (46XX), the fetus's body develops along what is considered the default path. In the thirteenth week, the gonads transform into ovaries. In the absence of testes producing male hormones, the sexual system develops along female lines. The Wolffian (male) ducts shrivel up. The typical sexual differentiation path is summarized in Table 2.

### Variations of Sex Development

Millions of people do not follow the typical sexual differentiation path and they have sex indicators that are not all clearly male or female. A number of variations from the typical sex development path could lead to the development of an intersex condition. This section describes some of the more common intersex conditions; a table summarizing these conditions appears in the appendix. Universal agreement about what conditions should be considered intersex does not exist. Some people believe that the term *intersex* should apply only to people with ambiguous genitalia or an unclear gender identity. Others have asserted that *intersex* should refer only to conditions in which the chromosomes and phenotype are discordant.

**TABLE 2**

*Typical Path of Sexual Differentiation*

|  | *Males* | *Females* |
|---|---|---|
| *Genetic/chromosomal sex* | XY | XX |
| *Gonadal sex:*<br>*Reproductive sex glands* | Testes | Ovaries |
| *External morphologic sex* | Penis and scrotum | Clitoris and labia |
| *Internal morphologic sex* | Seminal vesicles, prostate | Vagina, uterus, fallopian tubes |
| *Hormonal sex*<sup>*</sup> | Androgens | Estrogens |
| *Phenotypic sex*<br>*(secondary sex features)*<sup>**</sup> | Facial and chest hair | Breasts |
| *Assigned sex/gender*<br>*of rearing*<sup>***</sup> | Male | Female |
| *Gender identity* | Male | Female |

* Although androgens and estrogens are referred to as male and female hormones, respectively, all human sex hormones are shared by men and women in varying levels.

** Phenotypic sex characteristics may vary in different societies. For instance, facial hair in women is more accepted in some cultures and therefore is less associated with maleness. Similarly, the absence of chest hair and facial hair is not necessarily characterized as female in some cultures in which men typically have less facial and chest hair.

*** Assigned sex and gender of rearing are generally the same. Although it is rare, sometimes parents will raise a child in the gender opposite that assigned at birth. In addition, if a child exhibits a gender identity opposite to the sex assigned at birth, parents may begin to raise the child in the new gender role.

### Chromosomal Variations

Some individuals have chromosomes that vary from the typical XX/XY configuration. Chromosomal variations include XXX, XXY, XXXY, XYY, XYYY, XYYYY, and XO (denoting a single X chromosome). Two of the more common chromosomal variations include Klinefelter syndrome and Turner syndrome. Men with Klinefelter syndrome have one Y chromosome and two or more X chromosomes. Women with Turner syndrome have only one X chromosome.

*Gonadal Variations*

Some individuals have neither two testicles nor two ovaries. Variations include ovotestes (a combination of ovarian and testicular tissue), one testicle and one ovary, and streak gonads that do not appear to function as either ovaries or testicles. Pure gonadal dysgenesis is a condition sometimes referred to as Swyer syndrome. Individuals with Swyer syndrome have XY chromosomes but may be missing the sex-determining segment on the Y chromosome. Therefore, fetuses with this condition do not develop fully formed testes. In the absence of functioning testes, the fetus appears female but will not have a uterus and ovaries. Often this condition is not apparent at birth and is not diagnosed until puberty, when the absence of breast development and menstruation leads to a diagnosis.

*Hormonal Variations*

Some XY fetuses are unable to use the male hormones being produced by their testicles and therefore their bodies do not fully develop along the male path. For example, XY infants with complete androgen insensitivity syndrome (CAIS) have a problem with their androgen receptors. Because their bodies cannot process the androgens being produced by their testicles, these fetuses will develop along the default female path and will form external female genitalia. They will not develop female internal reproductive organs because the Mullerian inhibiting factor produced by the testes will inhibit the growth of the uterus and fallopian tubes. Often the vagina will be shorter than average. Sometimes this condition is diagnosed at birth, but occasionally diagnosis does not occur until puberty. People with CAIS have a female gender identity.

Instead of a complete insensitivity to androgens, some XY fetuses have partial androgen insensitivity syndrome (PAIS). Depending on the degree of receptivity to androgens, the external genitalia may be completely or partially masculinized.

The condition called 5 alpha reductase deficiency (5-ARD) results from the body's failure to convert testosterone to dihydrotestosterone, the more powerful form of androgen responsible for the development of male external genitalia in an XY fetus. Individuals with 5-ARD may appear to be females at birth. At the onset of puberty, the increased androgen levels may cause the body to masculinize. If masculinization occurs, the testes descend, the voice deepens, muscle mass substantially increases, and a "functional" penis that is capable of ejaculation develops from what was thought to be the clitoris.

Individuals with congenital adrenal hyperplasia (CAH) have XX chromosomes and ovaries. Due to a problem with the adrenal system, the fetus's body will masculinize. The external genitalia may be more similar to male genitals.

## The Medical Determinants of Sex Have Evolved

Although medical experts agree that many factors contribute to a person's sex, the attributes that have been used to differentiate men from women have varied over time and the issue is still a matter of great controversy.

### The Age of the Gonads: Late Nineteenth and Early Twentieth Centuries

In the late nineteenth and early twentieth centuries, sex was determined based on a person's gonads.[3] A person with testicles was considered a male and a person with ovaries was labeled female. During this time, scientists understood that male and female embryos begin with the same basic sexual features. They also knew that these sex attributes begin to differentiate in utero and continue to differentiate after birth. By the 1870s, scientists understood that the female fetus's gonads develop into ovaries and the male's gonads become testicles.

Although medical experts of this era knew that a variety of anatomical criteria could be used to determine a person's sex, they decided that the gonads should be the critical marker. Therefore, they declared that people with ovaries were women and people with testicles were men. This singular focus on gonadal tissue, to the exclusion of other known sex attributes, may have been influenced by the critical role that the gonads play in the reproductive process. The "Age of the Gonads" was short-lived. Within fifty years, the focus began to shift to another sex attribute: the genitalia.[4]

### The Age of the Genitalia: 1950s–1990s

By the middle of the twentieth century, medical experts had rejected the gonads as the "true" sex indicator and instead started to focus on the appearance of the external genitalia. Before the 1950s, if a newborn emerged with ambiguous genitalia, doctors would assign a sex to the infant that they believed was most appropriate and they would not otherwise surgically or hormonally alter the child.[5] During the middle of the twentieth century, two developments occurred that changed the manner in which medical experts determined sex. First, surgical techniques were developed that made it possible to modify genitalia to what was considered to be a "cosmetically acceptable" appearance. Second, the idea that gender identity was based on nurture and not nature became the conventional wisdom. In other words, most doctors, sociologists, and psychologists believed that children were born without an innate sense of being male or female.[6] Physicians developed a treatment approach based on the following three assumptions:

- Infants are born without an innate sense of gender. Therefore, infants can be raised as either boys or girls and they will develop the gender identity that matches their genitalia and the gender role in which they are raised.
- Children who grow up with atypical genitalia will suffer severe psychological trauma.
- A child's intersex condition is a source of shame and should be hidden from friends, family, and the child.

Thus, beginning in the 1950s, the standard protocol for treating newborns with ambiguous genitalia involved surgical alteration of "unacceptable" genitalia into "normal" genitalia. Normal genitalia for boys required an "adequate" penis. If doctors believed that an XY infant had an "adequate" penis, the child would be raised as a boy. A child without an "adequate" penis would be surgically altered and raised as a girl. The penis became the essential determinant of sex because medical experts believed that a male could only be a true man if he possessed a penis that was capable of penetrating a vagina and allowed him to urinate in a standing position. Medical technology at this time was capable of creating what was considered an adequate vagina (defined as one that was capable of being penetrated by an adequate penis), but the technology was not advanced enough to create a fully functional penis (one that was capable of penetrating a vagina). Therefore, surgeons would typically turn XY infants with small penises or infants with other genital ambiguity into girls.[7]

Under this protocol, XY infants with smaller penises were surgically and hormonally altered and raised as girls because of the dominant belief that growing up as a boy with an "inadequate" penis was too psychologically traumatic to risk. Some XY infants who had fully functional testicles had their ability to reproduce destroyed rather than having them be raised with a penis that was considered smaller than the norm. XX infants with a phallus that was more similar in length to a penis than a clitoris were treated differently. If they had the ability to bear a child as an adult, doctors would maintain their reproductive capacity. They would surgically remove the clitoris or reduce it to a size that they considered acceptable, even though the surgery might diminish or destroy the person's ability to engage in satisfactory sex.

In other words, the dominant protocol required that children should only be raised as males if as adults they would be able to engage in conventional sexual acts by penetrating a female's vagina. For females, however, the primary emphasis was on maintaining reproductive capacity rather than preserving the ability to enjoy sexual acts.[8]

Because infants with an intersex condition were considered "abnormal," their birth typically was shrouded in shame and secrecy. Doctors often told parents half truths about their children's conditions. Parents were also encouraged to lie to their children about the nature of their condition. The children were viewed as "freaks." Their conditions were to be studied by physicians and hidden from society.

Sherri Groveman Morris's description of growing up with complete androgen insensitivity syndrome captures the experiences of many people with an intersex condition treated under the standard protocol that began in the 1950s:

Sadly, my parents were not offered any type of emotional counseling to help them parse the distressing fact of having a child labeled, as my medical records show I was, a *pseudo-hermaphrodite*. Instead my diagnosis was considered a tragic mistake of nature by both my physicians and my parents. Given that I looked normal, however, my parents undoubtedly took solace in that they did not ever have to reveal the truth about my body to friends or relatives, and could keep it a secret even from immediate family members.

Having not had an opportunity to work through their own shame and guilt at having a child born with an intersex condition, my parents were even less able to develop any kind of game plan to disclose the details about such a fact to me. Instead they were advised by my pediatric endocrinologist to tell me I had a simple hernia when, as a young child, I discovered the abdominal scar (from removal of the testes soon after birth) just above my pubic region. They were then to say nothing again until the eve of puberty, at which time they should tell me that I had "twisted ovaries," which had been removed at birth to prevent them from becoming cancerous. . . .

By far the most disturbing of my recollections was of being on an examining table while interns and residents "inspected" me, all the while discussing the particulars of my anatomy in medical jargon I could not understand. Adolescence is an awkward body image time under the best of circumstances, and for those born with any physical anomaly, this awkwardness is undoubtedly compounded. But rather than mitigating my body image challenges, being put on display in this manner made me feel ashamed, freakish, and certainly "unfit for human consumption" in any sexual sense.[9]

## Challenges to the Traditional Treatment Protocol: 1990s–Present

During the 1990s, a number of people began to question the premises underlying the dominant treatment protocol for infants born with "ambiguous" genitalia. Many authorities, including experts in a variety of disciplines and intersex activist organizations, began to call for either a moratorium or a severe limitation on the practice of surgically altering infants with an intersex condition.[10] They challenged standard medical practices for three reasons:

- They believed that gender identity could not be manipulated by surgical and hormonal alteration. They asserted that these interventions could lead to irreversible harm if the child's gender identity did not develop in conformity with the surgically created genitalia. Therefore, they called for a moratorium on all surgeries that turned XY infants into girls based on the presumption that infants were born without an innate sense of gender.
- They argued that surgical interventions to create cosmetically acceptable genitalia, such as reducing the size of the clitoris, cause more physical and psychological trauma than does growing up with atypical genitalia. Many adults with an intersex condition who had been subjected to cosmetic genital surgery maintained that it often caused a loss or diminishment of erotic response, genital pain or discomfort, infections, scarring, urinary incontinence, and cosmetically unacceptable genitalia. Therefore, they advocated for a moratorium on all medically unnecessary cosmetic genital surgeries.
- They asserted that the dominant protocol, which was based on half truths and secrecy, caused psychological trauma because it exacerbated a person's sense of shame by reinforcing cultural norms of sexual abnormality. People with an intersex condition who were subjected to the standard treatment protocol experienced it as a sexual violation that led to a profound loss of their autonomy and extreme humiliation.

### Challenges to the Assumption That Gender Identity Is Completely Malleable

A number of recent studies on gender identity development indicate that gender identity may be more dependent on brain function and hormonal influences than on the appearance of the genitalia. In other words, the studies do not support the premise that children are born without an innate sense of gender. As a result, many physicians have abandoned the practice of surgically altering XY males with "inadequate" penises and assigning them to the female sex.

The report that has been cited most frequently to challenge the assumption of gender malleability was published in 1997 by Milton Diamond and Keith Sigmundson. Diamond and Sigmundson published a follow-up report on David Reimer, a male infant who had been surgically altered and raised as a female after a botched circumcision in infancy irreparably harmed his penis. Early reports about David indicated that he had happily adjusted to being raised as a girl, named Brenda. The earlier reports were exposed as false in Diamond and Sigmundson's 1997 article. Despite the surgical and hormonal intervention and being raised as a female, David had always thought of himself as a boy. As a teen, he chose to have surgery and hormonal treatment so that he could return to living as a male. In other words, despite the fact that David was told he was a girl, was raised as a girl, took female hormones, and had female genitalia and a female body, he still thought of himself as a boy.[11] Eventually, David married a woman and helped her raise her two children. Sadly, David committed suicide soon after his identical twin brother died of a drug overdose.

Other recent studies continue to confirm that gender identity is heavily influenced by prenatal influences and brain development and less dependent on physical attributes.[12] In 2004, William Reiner and John Gearhart published a study tracing the gender identity development of sixteen genetic males who were born with severe phallic inadequacy. Following the dominant treatment protocol at the time, fourteen of the sixteen children underwent surgical modification and were assigned the female sex. Two were raised as males without any surgical intervention. The study indicated that the two children who were raised as males had an unambiguous male identity. Of the fourteen children raised as females, five were living as females, three were living with unclear sexual identity (although two of the three had declared themselves male), and six were living as males. The researchers concluded that the appearance of the genitalia and the gender of rearing did not necessarily determine a person's gender self-identity. They found that the effect of prenatal androgens on the developing brain appear to be a major determinant of the formation of a male gender identity. Reiner and Gearhart acknowledged that more research is necessary to determine the exact process that leads to gender identity because "the specific mechanisms of the development of male sex itself remain largely unknown."[13]

Recent studies of the brains of transsexuals also support the idea that gender identity is likely related to brain development. Researchers studying the human hypothalamus have found it to be sexually dimorphic. Just as the fetus's rudimentary sex organs differentiate into "male" and "female" reproductive systems and genitalia, sex differences also can be seen in the human brain. When researchers examined the portion of the human hypothalamus that is understood to be sexually dimorphic, they found that the brains of male-to-female transsexuals were more similar to female brains than to male brains. The researchers concluded that sex differentiation of the brain sometimes goes in the opposite direction from the sexual development of the genitalia. In other words, gender self-identity may not comport with genital sex due to neurobiological factors that exist during fetal development.[14]

In 2005, an international multidisciplinary team of experts convened to revisit the treatment guidelines for infants with an intersex condition. In 2006, they published a "Consensus Statement on Management of Intersex Disorders" (2006 Consensus Statement), which recommends that physicians consider the following factors when suggesting a gender assignment for infants with an intersex condition: the etiology of the intersex condition, genital appearance, surgical options, the need for lifelong hormone replacement therapy, the potential for fertility, the views of the family, and sometimes the circumstances relating to cultural practices.[15] The report recognizes that appropriate gender assignment is not clear in all cases. In some intersex conditions, the dissatisfaction rate with the assigned gender may be as high as 25 percent.[16] Therefore, even under a best practices model based on current research, experts cannot predict with certainty the eventual gender identity of many infants with an intersex condition.

At this point, scientists do not fully understand exactly how chromosomes, brain structure, exposure to hormonal levels in utero, and familial and societal dynamics interact and contribute to gender identity formation. Now that most experts recognize that gender identity is not completely malleable and that genital appearance does not always predict gender identity accurately, surgeries to "create" a gender occur less frequently. Most doctors perform multiple tests to determine the likely gender identity of an infant born with an intersex condition and suggest that the parents raise the child in that gender role. Anecdotal evidence indicates, however, that some physicians will still surgically alter XY infants and will suggest that parents raise the children as girls if they do not believe they can create an "acceptable" penis.[17]

## Challenges to Medical Interventions to Create Cosmetically Acceptable Genitalia

Although surgeries to "create a gender" have diminished, doctors still frequently perform cosmetic genital surgeries to conform a child's genitalia to a binary sex norm. If a child with an intersex condition is going to be raised as a girl, often physicians will reduce the size of her clitoris if they believe it is too large. If a child with an intersex condition is going to be raised as a boy and the urethral opening appears someplace on the shaft rather than the tip of the penis, doctors may perform multiple surgeries to modify the penis.

Many physicians still conclude that allowing a child to grow up with atypical genitalia will lead to irreparable emotional and psychological trauma, despite the lack of studies to support that belief. In addition, some in the medical community believe that discordant gender features, such as male gonads nestled inside a girl's abdominal cavity, must be removed, despite the lack of evidence that they will cause harm and the existence of evidence that they may have beneficial effects.[18] In other words, despite the absence of any evidence linking cosmetic genital surgery with psychological well-being and medical benefit, these surgeries are still being performed.

A review of the recent literature on cosmetic surgeries to alter the genital appearance indicates that current practices vary widely. During the past ten years, experts have published a number of studies examining the effect of these cosmetic genital surgeries. Although these publications shed some light on the issue, they acknowledge that until long term comprehensive retrospective studies are conducted, no firm conclusions can be drawn about whether these interventions are beneficial or whether they lead to psychological harm and sexual dysfunction. Therefore, approaches will continue to be inconsistent.

Scientific publications during the past ten years illustrate the rapid pace at which the standard protocol for the treatment of infants with an intersex condition is changing. For example, in 2000, the American Academy of Pediatrics (AAP) published "Evaluation of the Newborn with Developmental Anomalies of the External Genitalia." At that time, the AAP still considered the birth of a child with an intersex condition to be a social emergency and presumed that early surgery, including clitoral reduction, vaginoplasty, removal of gonadal tissue, and surgical modification of the penis, should be performed within the first eighteen months of a child's life.[19]

Within a short time of the publication of that statement, a number of experts began to call for a moratorium on cosmetic genital surgeries on infants with an intersex condition. They maintained that these surgeries should no longer be performed because the surgeries are not medically necessary; the surgeries often result in scarring and pain; additional surgeries are often required; surgeries often interfere with sexual satisfaction; the children often suffer from stigma and trauma by being treated as abnormal and in need of fixing; medically unnecessary surgery should not be used to relieve the anxiety of the parents of the intersex child; and the children's sense of autonomy may be harmed when they are old enough to understand the procedure and its consequences.[20]

In 2001, a group of experts published a study of forty-four adolescent patients, all of whom had undergone cosmetic genital surgery in infancy between 1979 and 1995. They concluded that medically unnecessary cosmetic genital surgeries should be delayed until the child is old enough to make the decision.[21] Another study from the United Kingdom concluded from a study of fourteen patients with congenital adrenal hyperplasia (CAH) that the results of early surgery were disappointing and recommended that these surgeries generally be delayed until after puberty.[22]

In 2004, the Hastings Center, a well-respected nonpartisan organization that studies ethical standards in heath and medicine, convened a multidisciplinary group to consider the medical, psychosocial, and ethical issues associated with the care of children born with atypical genitalia. This group of experts concluded that it is unethical to perform surgery to normalize the appearance of the genitalia without the informed consent of the patient (the child). They determined that parental consent was not adequate to protect the child's interests. The group acknowledged that some surgeons maintain that technical considerations warrant some early surgeries, but they concluded that the irrevocable nature of the surgery warranted extreme caution and questioned whether surgical expediency could ever outweigh the psychosocial and ethical arguments for waiting until the children reach the age at which they can meaningfully participate in the decision.[23]

The 2006 Consensus Statement provides the most thorough analysis of the current treatment protocols for children with an intersex condition and recommends a number of changes to current practices. It encourages physicians to adopt a more cautious approach before undertaking surgical intervention. It suggests that clitoral reduction be limited to cases of severe genital virilization (the development of male sex characteristics in a female) and should not be performed on all clitorises that are larger than the norm. It also emphasizes that the focus of such surgeries should be on functional outcome (orgasmic function and erectile sensation) rather than purely on cosmetic appearance. It also acknowledges that absolutely no evidence exists to support the longstanding assumption that genital surgery carried out for cosmetic purposes during the first year of life relieves parental distress or improves the parent child bond.[24]

The 2006 Consensus Statement and its recommended guidelines have been applauded by many people and endorsed by the American Academy of Pediatrics, which retired the 2000 statement. The 2006 Consensus Statement, however, fails to resolve the issue at the heart of the current controversies: should medically unnecessary cosmetic genital surgeries ever be performed on infants? Some people have criticized the 2006 Consensus Statement for supporting surgery in case of severe virilization even though the current data do not support the conclusion that current surgical techniques preserve sensation.[25] Others have supported the 2006 Consensus Statement's affirmation of the parents' right to consent to genital surgery.[26] No studies have examined the effect that the 2006 Consensus Statement has had on current practices. Although recent reports all recognize that surgical alteration of infants with an intersex condition is problematic, one comprehensive study published in 2007 found that most parents still choose to consent to genitoplasty on behalf of their infants. Some parents, however, have elected to postpone the surgery until the child is old enough to participate in the decision.[27]

Surgical interventions are not the only technique doctors have relied on to produce cosmetically "acceptable" genitalia. Some doctors have also experimented with other methods of altering the appearance of the genitalia of infants with an intersex condition. For example, instead of performing surgery after the child is born, some doctors are administering drugs to pregnant mothers who may be carrying a child with one type of intersex condition, 21-hydroxylase deficiency congenital adrenal hyperplasia (CAH), an adrenal disorder that can lead to the formation of atypical genitalia.[28]

An XX fetus with CAH has adrenal glands that produce high levels of androgens, which are masculinizing hormones. Depending on the level of exposure, these children may be born with genitalia that have been partially masculinized. Some doctors are administering dexamethasone to pregnant women who are at risk of carrying a child with CAH because this drug has been proven effective in stopping the masculinization of the genitalia.[29]

This practice is problematic because it could cause significant harm to the fetus. Prenatal exposure to dexamethasone has been shown to cause brain changes.[30] Children who have been exposed have displayed problems with working memory, verbal processing, and anxiety.[31] Administering this drug is also problematic because it is exposing fetuses that will not be negatively affected by CAH to these dangers. Dexamethasone could potentially provide a benefit to about 10 percent of the fetuses being exposed to it because the drug will prevent the development of masculinized genitalia in XX fetuses.[32] But the goal of producing cosmetically acceptable genitalia is being sought at the expense of creating a significant risk of harm to the 90 percent of the fetuses that will receive absolutely no benefit. In addition, some reports have also indicated potential harm to the pregnant mother.[33]

### Challenges to Psychologically Harmful Practices

The intersex movement has been very successful in educating the medical community about the harm of telling parents half truths and lying to children. The 2006 Consensus Statement emphasizes the importance of open communication and participatory decision making. It encourages the use of a multidisciplinary treatment team, including psychologists, psychiatrists, social workers, and ethicists, who can adequately address the emotional aspects of the process. It also urges treating physicians to emphasize that intersexuality is not shameful and that children have the potential to become well-adjusted adults.[34]

Less attention has been paid to the psychological harm that can result from other common practices. Many children with an intersex condition have had their bodies and genitalia put on display and photographed so that doctors, residents, and interns could learn more about intersexuality.[35] A number of adults with an intersex condition have reported that childhood genital exams were psychologically harmful.[36] One person, who had not undergone genital surgery but had been subjected to numerous physical examinations, stated,

> The loss of control in having others comment and touch my body, while I was expected to lie still and silent, felt to me like rape. This was not done in furtherance of my "treatment," but rather in furtherance of an intern's medical education. Physician training is important, but can such examinations be justified if they leave the person feeling violated?[37]

Other medical practices that involve a significant risk of psychological trauma to children with an intersex condition continue. For example, one physician has used a cotton tip and vibrator to stimulate the clitoris, labia, and thighs of young girls and women who have undergone clitoral reduction surgeries. The purported purpose is to determine whether his surgeries have reduced the sensitivity of the clitoris.[38]

This testing has caused outrage among some experts.[39] When Kenneth Zucker, a psychologist who specializes in the treatment of intersexuality, heard about this practice, he stated,

> By age 6, 7, 8, kids don't even want to show their private parts to their parents. Certainly by age 8, 9, 10, the last few years of childhood, many children don't want to see their parents in the nude—and don't want their parents to see them in the nude. So now they're being taken to a doctor, who may have done very good surgery on them, who is applying this device to a very personal and private part of the body. I think that there are many risks in doing this under the guise of medical objectivity.[40]

People concerned about medical practices affecting children with an intersex condition have called for comprehensive long term retrospective studies to determine whether cosmetic genital surgery and other medical interventions are actually beneficial to the children subjected to these procedures. Until these studies are conducted, medical practices will continue to vary.

A number of experts in a variety of disciplines have challenged current practices because they are experimental, have not been proven to be beneficial, and are based on gender, sex, and disability stereotypes. Given these problems, some intersex activists have asserted that these invasive surgeries should not be performed without the informed consent of the patient (the child). The next chapter introduces the legal and medical doctrine of informed consent and analyzes whether the doctrine as currently applied adequately protects the rights of children born with an intersex condition.

# 2

# Who Has the Right to
# Choose My Sex and Genitalia?

*When Cheryl was born in 1956, she had genitalia that looked "like a little parkerhouse roll with a cleft in the middle and a little nubbin forward." Based on the doctors' recommendations, her parents raised her as a boy for eighteen months. At that point, doctors performing exploratory surgery discovered the presence of both ovarian and testicular tissue and they recommended that Cheryl's genitalia be surgically altered to a more "feminine" appearance and that she be raised as a girl. Her parents consented and physicians surgically removed Cheryl's phallus, which they decided was too large to qualify as a clitoris.*

*The surgery was so traumatic that Cheryl stopped speaking for about six months. For most of her childhood and young-adult life, she felt extraordinarily unhappy and isolated. By nineteen, she was filled with rage and had suicidal thoughts. Although she graduated from MIT, studied Japanese at Harvard University, and became a successful businesswoman, she remained emotionally tormented until she became an activist for the intersex community at age thirty-five.[1]*

Whether parents should have the power to approve surgical alteration of their infant's genitalia and reproductive systems is extremely controversial. Intersex activists and a growing group of medical experts believe that medically unnecessary cosmetic surgeries on infants born with an intersex condition should be severely curtailed or completely banned. Supporters of a complete moratorium believe that the traditional model is likely to cause severe trauma, including physical harm, emotional impairment, and stigmatization. They assert that a medical protocol that supports surgical intervention and emphasizes the "normalization" of an infant's genitalia will lead to parental guilt and shame about giving birth to an "abnormal" baby. More important, the attempt to "normalize" will reinforce the child's sense of stigma and exacerbate the child's sense of humiliation, sexual invasion, and loss of control.[2]

Those who support a moratorium also assert that relieving the parents' anxiety over their child's intersex condition should not be accomplished by surgically altering the child to fit societal norms. Instead, they emphasize that parents should be provided complete information about their child's condition and offered appropriate professional counseling and peer support. They assert that treatment of a child's intersex condition should be limited to conditions that pose an actual risk to the child's physical health. They believe that only the affected children, when they reach an age at which they are able to appropriately assess the risks and benefits, should have the power to decide whether they want to undergo surgery.[3]

In 2004, the National Endowment for the Humanities funded a project, Surgically Shaping Children, undertaken by the Hastings Center, to examine the ethical questions that arise when physicians surgically alter children to "normalize" their appearance. The working group, composed of experts in a variety of disciplines, unanimously condemned the performance of risky and painful surgeries that have not been proven to enhance sexual function or to produce a "normal" appearance. The group concluded that cosmetic genital surgeries should not be performed on children until they are able to meaningfully participate in the decision.[4]

Most doctors and parents, however, oppose a moratorium on infant genital cosmetic surgeries and believe that surgical alteration is in the best interests of a child born with an intersex condition. They are concerned that an untreated child may suffer psychological trauma from growing up with atypical-appearing genitalia. They believe this potential risk of psychological harm is more detrimental than the potential risks of surgery. They assert that parents should continue to be allowed to consent to these surgeries because they are in the best position to determine what treatment would be in their child's best interests.[5] This group believes that parents who are fully educated about all the risks and benefits of the different protocols should have the authority to determine what is in the best interests of their child.[6]

Although a significant minority of parents now decline or postpone surgery on their children with atypical genitalia, most parents still consent to the surgery.[7] As one parent posted on a message board, "How can anyone possibly think that a child can grow up and feel confident of her sexuality looking down at her genitals that look like a penis? Come on."[8]

Adults with an intersex condition also disagree about whether parents should have the ability to consent to these surgeries during their child's infancy. One study, published in 2004, surveyed seventy-two patients with XY chromosomes about a number of issues. Some of the surveyed patients had been raised as males and others had been raised as females. Not all had been subjected to surgery as infants and those who had been surgically altered had undergone a variety of surgical interventions. Although the majority of the group approved of genital surgery on infants born with atypical genitalia, a significant minority believed that such surgeries should not be performed without the informed consent of the person with the condition. The authors of the study recognized that their sample size was small and may not have been representative. They called for those who are in a position to control the guidelines for treatment of infants with an intersex condition to obtain additional data to determine the optimal treatment protocol.[9]

Until comprehensive retrospective studies are conducted that clearly establish whether surgical and hormonal alteration of an infant with an intersex condition is beneficial, these interventions will continue to be controversial. Given the critical interests at stake and the polarized nature of the debate, legal institutions will likely be brought into the dispute. Legislatures may be asked to enact statutes and in the absence of legislative action, courts may be asked to intervene. Thus far, no country or state has enacted controlling legislation and Colombia is the only jurisdiction in which the highest court has rendered an opinion on this issue.[10] Therefore, if courts are asked to resolve the legal, medical, and ethical issues surrounding consent to the treatment of children born with an intersex condition, the outcome is far from clear.

This chapter examines the relevant legal doctrines and potential legal approaches. It begins by introducing the right to autonomy and the requirement that medical procedures be undertaken only with proper informed consent. It then explains how the legal requirement of informed consent is applied to decisions made on behalf of children. It concludes by analyzing three proposed alternatives to the current informed consent procedures affecting children with an intersex condition:

1. Impose enhanced informed consent rules.
2. Delay all surgeries until children mature and can decide for themselves.
3. Impose some type of external oversight by a court or an ethics committee.

## The Right to Autonomy and the Requirement of Informed Consent

*Christiane Volling was born with ambiguous genitalia, but she was raised as a boy. The doctors believed that she was born with a mixture of male and female reproductive organs and when she was eighteen, they recommended that she undergo surgery. To the doctors' surprise, during the operation they discovered that she had normal ovaries and a uterus and no sign of internal male sex organs. Instead of ending the procedure, the doctors proceeded to remove her normal female reproductive organs. Christiane sued and sought damages for pain and suffering based on the physicians' failure to fully disclose to her the full extent of the consequences of her operation and all reasonable available alternatives. Thirty years after the operation was performed, a court in Germany ruled that "this invasive procedure should not have been performed without a full explanation." The court allowed her case to proceed to trial to determine the amount of damages.*[11]

The surgery performed on Christiane violates standard medical practices and legal rules requiring doctors to respect their patients' right to determine their medical treatment.[12] Patients' rights to autonomous decision making require that doctors (1) fully inform their patients about all material risks associated with any proposed medical treatment and (2) receive the patient's consent to the procedure. These requirements are referred to as the informed consent doctrine. The informed consent doctrine preserves patients' rights to make medical decisions on their own behalf. The doctrine protects an individual's right to bodily integrity and self-determination. The principle of autonomy requires deference to a patient's treatment choices, unless the government has a compelling interest that justifies overriding a competent person's right to autonomy. Courts rarely find such an overriding state interest.

## Informed Consent for the Medical Treatment of Children

The informed consent doctrine is premised on the patient's ability to understand and weigh the risks and benefits of the suggested procedure. Sometimes patients are unable to reach an informed decision because they are too young or they suffer from a disabling condition that precludes them from understanding the advantages and disadvantages of a procedure. In these cases, informed permission is required from a surrogate, typically the minor's (or incompetent's) parent(s).[13]

Parents' decisions on behalf of their children are generally accorded great deference for two reasons. First, legal institutions presume that parents will make decisions that are in the best interests of their children. In addition, the Constitution protects family privacy and parental authority.[14] Therefore, courts rarely become involved in parental medical decisions, as long as the parents and the physicians agree on the appropriate treatment.[15]

Typically, parents are allowed to consent to medical treatment for their minor children even if the treatment involves a significant risk of harm. Parents can consent to inoculations, complex surgeries, experimental treatments, radiation, chemotherapy, and other potentially harmful procedures. The law presumes that parents will weigh the potential benefits and risks of each procedure and make decisions that are in the best interest of their children.

In some circumstances, however, courts and legislatures have determined that complete deference to parental decisions may not be in a child's best interests. If the potential gravity of the consequences of the medical treatment is particularly severe and the situation involves potentially conflicting interests, courts may carefully review parents' consent to the treatment of their child. The classic cases requiring close scrutiny involve (1) terminating the life of a child in a persistent vegetative state, (2) authorizing an organ donation to benefit another family member (typically a sibling of the incompetent child), and (3) approving the involuntary sterilization of a minor or incompetent adult.

In these cases, courts do not simply defer to the parents. Instead, they require judicial oversight of these procedures for three reasons. First, these choices potentially infringe on constitutionally protected rights, including the right to life and the right to reproductive choice. Second, they involve a significant risk of harm to the children. Finally, parents may be in a position in which it is difficult for them to separate their child's interests from their own interests. For example, in the organ donation cases, parents are making a decision that may save the life of one child who requires a kidney transplant and at the same time expose their other child, the kidney donor, to a serious risk of harm. Similarly, in the involuntary sterilization cases, parents want to spare their child from the difficulties of bearing and rearing a child, but they may also be motivated by their concern about having to care for a grandchild should their incompetent child become pregnant or father a child. Therefore, courts will carefully scrutinize these decisions to ensure that the child's constitutional rights are protected and that any decision made is in the best interests of the child.[16]

In addition to termination of life, organ donation, and sterilization procedures, some jurisdictions have ruled that other invasive procedures, including involuntary psychosurgery, electroconvulsive therapy, and administration of antipsychotic medications, are life altering treatments that require additional measures to protect the child's rights.[17] Recently, the Washington Protection and Advocacy System (WPAS), a federally funded watchdog agency charged with investigating discriminatory treatment of people with a disability, investigated a case involving the administration of growth-attenuating hormones and the removal of the uterus and breast-bud tissue from a developmentally disabled child. The WPAS determined that these types of procedures, because they were invasive and irreversible, also required court supervision.[18]

## Parental Consent to the Surgical Alteration of Children with an Intersex Condition

Allowing parents to consent to cosmetic genital surgery on an infant with an intersex condition involves similarly complex issues. Currently, parents can consent to these surgeries and they are not subject to an external oversight or approval. Based on the important interests at stake, courts or legislatures could be convinced to place stricter limitations on the circumstances under which these procedures can be performed. The extent of the regulation would depend on many factors. The most important consideration would be whether the procedure affects a constitutionally protected right.

### Medical Procedures Resulting in Sterilization Affect the Constitutionally Protected Right to Reproduce and Require Strict Oversight

Legal rules governing sterilization in the United States have changed dramatically. During the first half of the twentieth century, it was commonplace to sterilize people with developmental disabilities. In 1927, the United States Supreme Court supported this practice in *Buck v. Bell*, with its controversial assertion that "[t]hree generations of imbeciles are enough."[19] In 1942, in *Skinner v. Oklahoma*, the Supreme Court began to impose strict restrictions on sterilization practices. The Court ruled that procreative choice is a fundamental human right protected by the United States Constitution. Thus, the Court limited the circumstances under which states could sterilize people without their consent.[20]

After *Skinner*, states adopted a variety of statutes regulating sterilization practices to ensure that a person's reproductive capacity would not be terminated inappropriately. These regulations typically require judicial oversight and approval of sterilizations performed on people who are not capable of consenting to the procedure themselves. Full protection of reproductive rights requires that before the sterilization is performed, a judge approves the procedure. During the judicial hearing, the child who will be subjected to sterilization must have a separate legal representative who advocates zealously on the child's behalf.[21]

Court approval is clearly required when the sole purpose of the procedure is sterilization. If the main reason for the medical treatment is something other than sterilization (e.g., removal of a cancerous growth) and sterilization is a byproduct, many doctors and attorneys believe that they can proceed without court approval. The WPAS, however, has concluded that all sterilizations of developmentally disabled individuals, regardless of the primary motivation for the procedure, should be approved by the court.[22]

Reproductive rights are compromised in a number of medical procedures performed on infants with an intersex condition. A number of current medical practices have the potential to destroy reproductive capacity. For example, if a child with CAH is to be raised as a male, doctors remove the child's female reproductive organs and thus destroy the child's ability to reproduce. In addition, doctors will also remove the testicles of infants with complete androgen insensitivity syndrome, which could potentially affect the children's future ability to reproduce.[23] Finally, although the practice is no longer supported in the medical literature, anecdotal evidence indicates that some doctors may still recommend raising an XY child with an "inadequate" penis as female and if the parents agree, the doctors will remove the child's testicles and end his ability to reproduce.

Although the sterilization statutes and cases have only addressed children with developmental disabilities, the principles relied on and the rules adopted in these actions should apply with equal force to prohibit the sterilization of a child with an intersex condition.[24] In fact, sterilizations of infants born with an intersex condition could be considered less justifiable than sterilizations of profoundly disabled children. When infants with an intersex condition mature, they will be able to provide their informed consent to a procedure, whereas profoundly disabled children will never be in a position to provide informed consent. Thus, the justification for sterilizing infants with an intersex condition is even less defensible.

Sterilizations of infants with an intersex condition will eventually be reviewed by courts. First, doctors or hospitals who are concerned about potential liability may seek court approval before they proceed with interventions that involve sterilization.[25] In addition, people who have had their reproductive ability terminated without their consent may initiate a lawsuit. Finally, governmental agencies could initiate investigations into these practices. When these lawsuits arise, courts should ban these types of procedures unless there is clear evidence that the sterilization would be in the child's best interests and that waiting until the child is old enough to make a decision would cause irreparable harm.

### Invasive and Irreversible Procedures Not Causing Sterilization May Require Similar Safeguards and Oversight

Procedures that do not affect reproductive capacity do not involve the same fundamental rights and, as a result, are not entitled to the same constitutional protection. Generally, parents' rights to make medical decisions on behalf of their minor children are respected. Typically, if parents consent to a medically recommended procedure, their decision is not subject to any type of review.[26]

Not all parental decisions are granted automatic deference. Although legal authority is sparse, some disability organizations have asserted that judicial approval is required for parental consent in cases involving invasive and irreversible procedures other than sterilization. For example, in a recent investigation involving the removal of the uterus and breast-bud tissue and the administration of hormones to a developmentally disabled child, the WPAS determined that these types of procedures should only be undertaken with court supervision.[27] In its extensive report, the WPAS stated,

> [T]he rights of parents to make treatment and other decisions for their minor children, however, are not unfettered. "[T]he state has a wide range of power for limiting parental freedom and authority in things affecting the child's welfare" [citing Prince v. Massachusetts, 321 U.S. 158 (1944)]. Parents generally have the right to make medical decisions for their minor children and provide informed consent for various procedures; however, courts have limited this authority when parents seek highly invasive and/or irreversible medical treatment of their minor children. [citing Parham v. J.R., 442 U.S. 584, 585 (1979)]. Courts and the Washington State Legislature, for example, have held that parents do not have the authority to consent to medical treatment in

cases involving involuntary inpatient psychiatric care, [citing Parham v. J.R., 442 U.S. 584 (1979) and T.B. v. Fairfax Hosp. Wash., 129 Wn. 2d 439, 452–453 (1996)], the administration of electro convulsive therapy in non-emergency life-saving situations [citing In re A.M.P., 303 Ill. App. 3d 907, 914–915, 708 N.E.2d 1235, 1240–1241 (1999); RCW 71.34.355(9)], psychosurgery [citing RCW 71.34.355(10)], abortions for mature minors [citing State v. Koome, 84 Wn. 2d 901, 909–910 (1975)], sterilization [citing In re Hayes, 93 Wn. 2d 228 (1980); In re K.M., 62 Wn. App. 811 (1991); In re Mary Moe, 432 N.E.2d 712, 716–717 (Mass. 1982); In re Rebecca D. Nilsson, 471 N.Y. Supp. 2d 439 (1983)], and other similar invasive medical treatments [citing State v. Baxter, 134 Wn. App. 587, 141 P.3d 92 (2006), denying a father the right to circumcise his eight year old son with a hunting knife], particularly where the interest of the parent may not be the same as those of the child [citing In re Hayes, 93 Wn. 2d 228, 236 (1980) and State v. Koome, 84 Wn. 2d 901, 904 (1975)].[28]

Many procedures performed on infants with an intersex condition have the potential to make orgasm difficult or impossible and may cause serious long term medical complications. These invasive and potentially irreversible surgeries can permanently and dramatically infringe on the right of people with an intersex condition to bodily integrity and sexual self-determination. In addition, safeguards are needed because parents may be making decisions at a time when they are suffering distress about giving birth to and raising an "abnormal" child. Under these circumstances, it is difficult for parents to objectively determine the treatment that would be in their child's long term best interests, especially because the issue may affect sexuality when the child becomes an adult. Thus, these procedures should only be allowed under conditions that ensure that the child's rights are protected.[29]

## Three Proposed Solutions

Three approaches have been proposed that would provide greater protection to the rights of children born with an intersex condition.

1. Allow parents to continue to control the decision but only under enhanced informed consent procedures.
2. Delay all medically unnecessary surgeries until children mature and can make their own decision.
3. Allow the surgeries to continue but impose some type of oversight by a court or an ethics committee.

## Impose an Enhanced Informed Consent Standard

Only one high court, the Constitutional Court of Colombia, has directly ruled on whether parents can consent to cosmetic genital surgery being performed on infants with an intersex condition.[30] Because of a court decision in 1995, doctors in Colombia were concerned about potential liability for performing genital surgery on infants with an intersex condition. Doctors in two cases recommended that the children they were treating undergo cosmetic genital surgery, but the doctors who made the recommendation refused to proceed without a court order. The parents of the two children sought court authority for the procedures to occur.

The Constitutional Court of Colombia considered evidence that supported the traditional model as well as evidence that criticized this model and supported a moratorium on cosmetic genital surgeries on infants with an intersex condition. The court concluded that the uncertain and conflicting evidence put the law at an impasse. The court reasoned that prohibiting surgery until the children reach the age of consent would be engaging in social experimentation, but allowing the surgery to continue under the standard protocol would not ensure that the best interests of the children were protected.

The Colombian court decided that surgical modification of an infant with an intersex condition must be treated differently from other types of parental consent cases. The court decided that the traditional informed consent rules do not guarantee that parents are in the best position to make a decision on behalf of their child. The court was concerned because (1) parents typically lack information about intersexuality, (2) intersexuality is viewed as a disease that must be cured, and (3) treating physicians frequently convey a false sense of urgency to provide a quick cure. The Colombian court recognized that under these circumstances, parents cannot easily distinguish their own fears and concerns from considerations of the "best interests" of their child. The court concluded that parents may approve these surgeries to "normalize" their children, who they view as "strange beings."[31]

The Colombian court decided to follow a middle path to protect the human rights of infants. It struck a balance between allowing parents full autonomy to consent to surgical alteration on behalf of their infant and barring all such surgeries. The court called on legal and medical institutions to establish "qualified and persistent" informed consent procedures that protect the rights of the child with an intersex condition until comprehensive studies clearly establish the course of treatment that is in the child's best interests.[32]

The court held that to meet the "qualified and consistent informed consent" requirements the following conditions must be met:

1. The consent must be in writing.
2. The information provided must be complete. The parents must be informed about the dangers of current treatments, the existence of other paradigms, and the possibility of delaying surgeries and giving adequate psychological support to the children.
3. The authorization must be given on several occasions over a reasonable time period to ensure the parents have enough time to truly understand the situation.[33]

## Delay All Procedures until the Child Matures and Can Meaningfully Participate in the Decision

A number of experts and people with an intersex condition who were subjected to surgery as infants have argued that given the significant and irreversible effects of these surgeries, no one other than the person undergoing the procedure should have the power to determine whether it should be performed. They have argued that a complete moratorium should be imposed on all medically unnecessary cosmetic genital surgeries on infants. They believe that these surgeries should be delayed until the children reach an age at which they can decide for themselves whether to undergo surgical alteration.[34]

If older minors decide that they would like to undergo any of these procedures, they would not have to be delayed until adulthood. Generally, minors are unable to provide legal consent, but the medical profession recognizes that adolescents (especially older adolescents) may have decision making abilities that are as well developed as those of adults.[35] Therefore, before treating an adolescent, physicians are encouraged to obtain patient assent to the parental consent. In some circumstances, depending on the age of the child, the procedure involved, and whether the adolescent has the legal ability to consent to a medical procedure, no parental approval is necessary.[36]

## Require Oversight by a Court or an Ethics Committee

Some critics of current practices who believe that cosmetic genital surgery on infants should be allowed to continue, but under more protective guidelines, have argued that allowing parents to control the decision does not ensure that the rights of the child with an intersex condition will be adequately protected. Given the nature of the rights at stake and the potential that these surgeries will lead to physical harm and emotional trauma, they have recommended that a court or a hospital ethics committee be brought into the decision making process. If a committee is used, it could consist of physicians, psychologists, adults with an intersex condition, and parents of children with an intersex condition. These committees could be beneficial because they would have access to all the relevant information, would consist of people who are not emotionally involved in the decision, and could provide support and referrals to the parents. Alternatively, the decision could be supervised by an independent court.[37]

## Potential Problems with the Three Proposals

Parents' decisions about cosmetic genital surgery on their infants and other medical treatments that have the potential to profoundly affect their children involve complex ethical issues. Some people favor complete deference to the parents, who they believe are in the best position to determine what will benefit their children. Others believe that these surgeries should be performed only with the informed consent of the patient, and not the patient's parents. Some assert that additional safeguards should be mandatory to ensure that the best interests of the child are paramount. No ideal solution exists; each of the three proposals presents potential problems.[38]

### Parental Consent under an Enhanced Informed Consent Standard

Improving the informed consent process may not resolve all the problems inherent in these procedures. Anne Tamar-Mattis, the executive director of Advocates for Informed Choice, has noted that even if informed consent procedures are improved, three problems would remain. First, parents may not be in a position to adequately consider the long term interests of their child. Second, the informed consent procedures may not adequately address the cultural biases (based on heteronormativity and sex/gender binary constructs) inherent in these decisions. Finally, parents may consent for personal reasons, such as their own discomfort or embarrassment over raising a child with atypical genitalia. Therefore, merely improving the informed consent practices may not adequately protect the children undergoing these operations.[39]

Studies suggest that parents may be more likely to choose cosmetic genital surgery for their children than the children would be once they mature. Parents may be more likely to underemphasize the importance of sexual gratification to their child and overemphasize their child's need to fit into societal norms.

In one study, female college students were asked to imagine that they had been born with a clitoris larger than one centimeter at birth. An overwhelming 93 percent of the students reported that they would not have wanted their parents to agree to surgery to alter the appearance of their genitalia. The students were more likely to want surgery to reduce a large nose, ears, or breasts than surgery to reduce an enlarged clitoris. This result is consistent with the women's ratings of the importance of genital sensation and capacity to orgasm, which they ranked as very important as compared to the size of the clitoris, which was ranked as only somewhat important.[40]

This same study asked male college students about their wishes if they had been born with a "micropenis," measuring less than two and a half centimeters at birth. They were asked whether they would have wanted to be raised as a boy with a small penis or surgically altered and reassigned female. More than half of the males rejected gender reassignment and surgical alteration. When the surgery was described as potentially reducing pleasurable sensitivity or orgasmic capability, they almost unanimously rejected surgery and opted to be raised as a boy with a small penis.[41]

The women and men in this study both reported that they did not believe that growing up with an enlarged clitoris or a small penis would have affected their sexual relations, peer and parent relations, and self-esteem.

In contrast, a recent study questioning parents about their priorities indicates that parents tend to emphasize their child's genital appearance over their child's erotic responsiveness. The study asked parents of children born with an intersex condition to rank the importance of sexual responsiveness and genital appearance. Ninety-five percent of the parents indicated that they would have authorized genital surgery for their child with an intersex condition, even if a reduction in sexual responsiveness was certain.[42]

Therefore, allowing parents to continue to consent to these procedures is problematic. Although parents may truly believe that they are choosing the option that they think will be most beneficial to their children, it is highly questionable whether they are able to accurately assess their children's priorities when they mature. Although most adults state that they would prioritize their erotic response over genital appearance, most parents believe that "normal" appearance and not potential erotic response would be more important to their child's well-being.

## Delay Medically Unnecessary Procedures until the Children Are Old Enough to Meaningfully Participate in the Decision

Delaying the decision until children reach adolescence, when they can participate in the decision making process, or adulthood, when they can legally consent, shows greater respect for their right to autonomy and privacy. Given the fact that no comprehensive studies exist that prove that delaying these surgeries leads to a better psychological outcome, courts may be hesitant to completely ban these procedures on young children.

Allowing adolescents to make these types of decisions respects their right to autonomy, but it may not necessarily lead to the optimal outcome. Given today's societal focus on appearance, adolescents may not be in a position to access accurately what their priorities will be as sexually active adults.

Cosmetic genital surgery has burgeoned into a booming business and is being offered to women who are dissatisfied with the shape, size, or proportions of their vulvas. Dozens of advertisements offer cosmetic genital surgery to conform female genitalia to an idealized norm.[43] According to two doctors who specialize in the treatment of women with an intersex condition, elective genitoplasty is fueled by women's misguided assumptions about what is considered to be "normal" genitalia.[44] Impressionable teenagers may be persuaded that cosmetic appearance overshadows sexual functioning. The other alternative, forcing people with intersex conditions to wait until they reach adulthood, however, may unnecessarily cause severe emotional or psychological trauma.

## Grant Decision Making Authority to a Court or an Ethics Board

Bringing in outside decision makers may ensure that the process is more informed, but granting decision making power to other individuals or groups may not necessarily result in a decision that accurately reflects the best interests of the child.

Judges are sometimes ill equipped to render decisions in these matters. They are not authorities on any of the medical or critical psychological issues at stake. In addition, judges may let their own biases affect the decision making process. The case that best illustrates the problems that may arise if this issue is litigated in the courts is a 1993 decision from the family court in Australia, *In re A*.[45]

*A was born with congenital adrenal hyperplasia (CAH) and had been raised as a girl. At puberty, A began to virilize and he self-identified as a boy. When A was fourteen and a half years old, he sought surgical treatment to bring his physical appearance in line with his gender identity. No one opposed the procedure. A's desire was supported by his parents and the medical treatment team, which included a surgeon, an endocrinologist, a psychiatrist, and a psychologist. Because the procedure would result in the sterilization of A, court approval was sought.*

*The court determined that although A had a general understanding of the problems involved with the proposed surgery, the court was not convinced that he was sufficiently mature to fully appreciate and objectively assess the various options. The court also decided that the parents did not have the power to consent on behalf of their child and that the treatment decision required court supervision. The court decided that court authorization was necessary as a "procedural safeguard" because it was not clear which decision would be in the child's best interests and an incorrect decision would yield particularly grave results.*

*Although the court decided that granting A's request was the correct decision, the court seriously considered denying the petition. The court stated, "It is clear on all the material that the various treating experts regard this . . . as being highly desirable in A's interests. I had nevertheless considered the possibility of rejecting the application on the basis that it is only another three and a half years until A attains 18 years and at that stage it would be open to him to make his own decision."[46]*

The court ultimately relied on the psychologist's evidence that delaying the surgery for three years posed a significant risk that A would commit suicide or suffer severe and irreparable psychological trauma. This possibility caused the court to grant A's petition. It is unclear how many other judges would have substituted their own judgment for that of the affected parties. Given that the judge in *In re A* was sorely tempted, this possibility cannot be ignored. Because judges are unlikely to have the knowledge to decide these issues and these requests may force judges to confront their own stereotypes about sex and gender, allowing one judge to determine the appropriate treatment for a child with an intersex condition may not always be ideal.

Even experts who have experience working with adolescents who are seeking genital-modification surgery may allow their biases to affect their decisions. For example, one surgeon who treats people with an intersex condition opined that a fourteen-year-old is old enough to understand the consequences of the decision to have genital surgery. He stated, "Now that's the perfect situation. There you've got a person who has declared exactly what they want. They're of an age where they understand the implications of the operation." But the same surgeon believed that a sixteen-year-old transsexual youth should not have the same right to agree to a similar surgery: "I don't know about the ethics of, of medical practitioners assisting transgender, transsexual processes in people who are under age. . . . Aren't you concerned about the ethics of 16 year olds? I mean because the brain in a 16 year old is a very, you know here today, gone tomorrow phenomenon. . . . I don't think that a 16 year old has the capacity to take that sort of decision."[47]

Referral to an ethics committee that is able to gather expert opinions from diverse sources is most likely to illuminate the risks and benefits of the various treatment options. Committee decisions on emotionally laden controversial issues, however, are also subject to problems. Studies have found that committee decisions are not always objective and they may not prioritize the needs of the patient.[48]

### A Fourth Alternative: Require an Ethics Committee Recommendation and Court Approval

Given the inherent problems in all these models, a more effective alternative may be to adopt a two-step approach that would involve an ethics committee and a court proceeding. Ethics committees consisting of experts from the relevant disciplines, including endocrinologists, pediatricians, psychologists, and sociologists, as well as adults with an intersex condition who have experienced the different treatment protocols and parents who have been faced with this decision, could serve four critical needs:

- They could provide guidance to the parents.
- Their opinions could provide expertise and guidance to the court.
- They could gather data on the outcomes of different treatment models.
- They could provide continuing education to people with an intersex condition, parents, and treating physicians.

After the ethics committee issues an advisory opinion, a court order would be required to approve any procedure to ensure the protection of the child's rights. An advocate for the child would need to be appointed to represent the interests of the child during the court proceeding. Before a court could approve any medical treatments, those seeking the procedure would be required to clearly show that the expected benefit to the child outweighs the risks, the proposed treatment is the least intrusive means available to obtain the benefit, and the interests of the child (as opposed to the interests of the parents) are the paramount concern.[49] This two-step process might be the most effective means to assure that any decisions made on behalf of children are in their best interests.

This approach would ensure that the decision maker is fully informed and that the positive and negative effects on the child are completely explored. This proposal is a compromise position between granting full authority to the parents and imposing a complete moratorium. It could be subject to criticism, however, from both sides. Those who believe that the state should not be interfering in parental rights would assert that parents are allowed to make other medical decisions involving even life-and-death matters (such as orders not to resuscitate) without interference from the state. Therefore, they should also be allowed to make the decision about whether to have their child undergo surgery. On the other hand, those who favor a moratorium would argue that allowing these surgeries to continue even with a court order does not adequately respect the child's right to autonomy.[50]

Ensuring that the fundamental rights of a child born with an intersex condition are adequately protected requires medical and legal institutions to review current informed consent practices. If the procedure results in sterilization, court approval should be obtained. If the procedure does not result in sterilization but is irreversible and invasive, legal institutions should consider whether additional safeguards should be imposed. Legislatures and courts could adopt rules banning infant genital surgery, requiring improvements in the informed consent procedures, or requiring external supervision or approval of these medical procedures by ethics committees and/or courts.

# PART II

## Gender Bending

# 3

# Legal Reinforcement
# of Gender Norms

Part I of this book explains and critiques the medical treatment protocol that emphasizes the importance of surgically altering the bodies of infants with an intersex condition so that they conform to a medically created binary sex norm. Part II focuses on the legal reaction to those who challenge or bend sex and gender norms.

"In 1843 Levi Suydam, a 23-year-old resident of Salisbury, Connecticut, asked the town's board of selectmen to allow him to vote as a Whig in a hotly contested local election. The request raised a flurry of objections from the opposition party, for a reason that must be rare in the annals of American democracy: It was said that Suydam was 'more female than male,' and thus (since only men had the right to vote) should not be allowed to cast a ballot. The selectmen brought in a physician, one Dr. William Barry, to examine Suydam and settle the matter. Presumably, upon encountering a phallus and testicles, the good doctor declared the prospective voter male. With Suydam safely in their column, the Whigs won the election by a majority of one.

"A few days later, however, Barry discovered that Suydam menstruated regularly and had a vaginal opening. Suydam had the narrow shoulders and broad hips characteristic of a female build, but occasionally 'he' felt physical attractions to the 'opposite' sex (by which 'he' meant women). Furthermore, 'his feminine propensities, such as fondness for gay colors, for pieces of calico, comparing and placing them together, and an aversion for bodily labor and an inability to perform the same, were remarked by many.' (Note that this 19th-century doctor did not distinguish between 'sex' and 'gender.' Thus he considered a fondness for piecing together swatches of calico just as telling as anatomy and physiology.) No one has yet discovered whether Suydam lost the right to vote. Whatever the outcome, the story *conveys both the political weight our culture places on ascertaining a person's correct 'sex' and the deep confusion that arises when it can't be easily determined.*"[1]

If the intersex movement is successful at stopping cosmetic genital surgeries on infants born with an intersex condition, when these children reach adulthood, they may be confronted with the same legal problems that plagued Suydam and confront transsexuals: state control over the determination of their legal sex. State sex determination actions could arise in two scenarios. First, people with sex attributes that are not clearly male or female may have their legal sex challenged by the state or other individuals. Second, people with an intersex condition may seek to change the sex indicated on their legal documents because it does not comport with their gender self-identity. Both of these scenarios may lead to state intervention.

Until sex reassignment surgery became available in the latter part of the twentieth century, legal institutions were rarely asked to determine whether a person qualified as a man or a woman. Although people with an intersex condition appear in ancient Greek mythology, early religious tracts, and English writings from the sixteenth century, legal institutions did not begin to wrestle seriously with this issue until the 1970s.

Ironically, a person's legal sex is significantly less important now than it has been at any other time in history. Before the second half of the twentieth century, the legal rights and obligations of men and women differed dramatically. During the past forty years, however, legislatures in the United States and other Western countries have repealed laws that differentiate between men and women, and courts have declared that most sex based laws are unconstitutional. The days in which women were barred from voting, serving on juries, and entering certain occupations are becoming a distant memory.

In the United States, governmental distinctions between men and women remain in only two significant areas: marriage restrictions and military rights and obligations. In addition to these legal distinctions, society reinforces the gender divide and imposes sex based differences in school and work dress codes, participation in athletic events, and sex segregation in locker rooms, bathrooms, and some housing.

The gradual disappearance of sex based distinctions in our laws reflects the partial blurring of gender and sex differences in our society. Although the range of acceptable behavior and dress requirements for men and women have become less discrete, societal and legal norms are still based on a binary system that presumes that only two sexes exist and that people fit neatly into either the *male* or the *female* category. In other words, a binary sex model still prevails and the state plays a role in determining who qualifies for legal status as a male or a female.[2]

Just as the medical determinants of sex have changed over time, the legal definitions of *male* and *female* have also varied. The legal determinants of sex have not necessarily reflected the scientific and medical advances that have enhanced our understanding of sex determination. Many legal institutions—including legislatures in more than twenty European countries, the European Court of Human Rights, the European Court of Justice, courts in Australia and New Zealand, and some state courts and legislatures in the United States—rely on scientific developments to guide them in their formation of the rules for determining a person's legal sex. Other legal institutions, including many U.S. state courts, rely on a variety of other factors. Some recent decisions have ignored scientific developments about gender identity formation in favor of the definition in *Webster's* dictionary, references to "our Creator," and outdated court rulings that do not reflect the current scientific understanding of sex differentiation. In addition, the legal determinants of sex may vary depending on the issue before the court. For example, courts and legislatures may adopt different tests for determining legal sex for purposes of marriage, identity documents, and housing.

Part II of the book explains how legal sex is determined for people with an intersex condition and for transsexuals in the three major areas where this issue has been litigated. Chapter 4 explores the major impetus for sex distinctions, protecting marriage as a heterosexual institution. Marriage cases in which the legal sex of one of the spouses is at issue is the context where most of the sex determination litigation has arisen. Chapter 5 discusses whether people with an intersex condition and transsexuals should be able to create their own legal identity through the name and sex indicator they choose for their official documents. Chapter 6 examines how housing and bathroom use rules are imposed on people who do not fit into the binary norm.[3]

These chapters illustrate the weaknesses of the tests that states have adopted for sex determination. Under the current legal system, a person's legal sex could change as a state line is crossed. In addition, a person's legal sex can vary within a state depending on whether the state is determining the ability to marry, to use public restrooms, or to a carry a driver's license or other official document with a name and sex indicator that match the person's gender identity.

# 4

# Can I Marry a Man,
# a Woman, Either, or Neither?

*Caroline and Dennis married on February 4, 1967. Three years later, they adopted Rebecca and on November 12, 1973, Caroline gave birth to Kyle. Although Kyle and Rebecca are not Dennis's biological children, Dennis would be their legal father if his marriage to Caroline is valid under Australian family law. Caroline and Dennis raised the children together until May 1979. At that time, Caroline sought to have the marriage annulled on the grounds that Dennis was not a man and thus the marriage was never legal.*

*When Dennis was born, he was identified as a male. He was raised as a boy, self identified as a male, and until puberty was viewed by society as a male. Sometime around the age of thirteen, Dennis's breasts began to develop. At sixteen, he began to have a monthly discharge of blood. Eventually, his breasts became so large that they aroused the curiosity and interest of his fellow workers, who frequently mocked Dennis and ridiculed his female-like qualities. These bodily changes caused Dennis great distress and embarrassment. Eventually he consulted a doctor, who performed surgery and discovered that Dennis had internal female organs, including an ovary and uterus. Dennis underwent four surgical operations to remove his internal female organs and breasts and to bring his external sex organs more into conformity with traditional male genitalia. Dennis met Caroline shortly after he completed these operations and they dated for five years before they married.*

*When Caroline sought an annulment after being married to Dennis for twelve years, the Family Law Court issued the annulment and ruled that a true marriage could not have occurred because Dennis was neither a man nor a woman but was a combination of both. In other words, the court determined that Dennis, as a nonman/nonwoman, did not have the legal right to marry at all.[1]*

Dennis's story is not fictional. In 1979, the Australian Family Court ruled that for purposes of marriage Dennis was neither a man nor a woman. This decision has been roundly criticized and will no longer be followed in Australia. In fact, it is unlikely that any jurisdiction would now bar a person with an intersex condition or a transsexual from marrying at all, but whether Dennis could legally marry a man or a woman is still far from clear.

The most recent published marriage case involving a wife with an intersex condition was decided in England in 2000. The judge who presided over the case wrote a twenty-four-page opinion in which he struggled with how to determine the wife's legal sex for purposes of marriage.[2]

*When Whitney was born in 1947, the doctors were unsure whether she should be registered as a boy or a girl. They left the decision to the parents, who decided to register her as male and raise her as a boy. When Whitney was two years old, a cousin adopted Whitney and continued to raise her as a boy. From an early age, Whitney preferred to play with dolls and wear girl's clothing. At secondary school, she refused to wear the boys' uniform or shower with the boys. By the time Whitney was fifteen years old, she had noticeable breasts and a female body shape. At this point, Whitney's adoptive father convinced Whitney's doctor to administer testosterone to Whitney to masculinize her body. Whitney objected and her father held her down so that the doctor could give her the shots. These injections had no effect and when her father suggested that they increase the frequency and size of the dosage and perform surgery to remove her breasts, Whitney ran away from home. She was found and forcibly returned. Two years later, she ran away again and never returned home.*

*Although Whitney sought surgery to feminize her body when she was twenty-three years old, she was unable to undergo surgical procedures at that time due to another medical problem. In 1987, Whitney underwent surgery to feminize her body. In 1993, Whitney married William. They separated three years later and William sought a declaration that the marriage was invalid, alleging that Whitney was not a woman.*

*No medical expert could testify as to the exact nature of Whitney's genitalia before her feminizing surgery. The physician who had performed the feminizing surgery was unable to provide a detailed description. The expert who testified at the time of trial reviewed the scant medical records and concluded that Whitney likely had partial androgen insensitivity syndrome (PAIS). Thus, Whitney had male (XY) chromosomes and was probably born with testicles, but her genitalia at birth were neither clearly male nor*

*female. The expert then concluded that it was a "close call" on the infor-*
*mation whether Whitney's phallus should be classified as a micropenis or a*
*clitoris.*

*The court asked Whitney to provide detailed evidence about the appear-*
*ance of her genitalia before the surgery was performed. She was questioned*
*about the size of her phallus, the existence of testicles and scrotal sac, whether*
*she had a vagina, the location of the opening of her urethra, and whether she*
*ever urinated in a standing position. The court acknowledged that Whitney*
*likely suffered embarrassment and discomfort about being asked to provide*
*this evidence. Despite Whitney's reticence to provide detailed information*
*about the appearance of her genitalia, the court found this information criti-*
*cal to its determination. In its findings, the court felt the need to provide a*
*detailed description of Whitney's genitalia and specifically located her ure-*
*thral opening "at, or near, the end or tip of the flap of skin" that would have*
*been considered her phallus.*

*The judge eventually determined that Whitney was legally a woman*
*for purposes of marriage, basing his decision on three criteria: her sex fac-*
*tors, her history and the medical evidence, and her ability to consummate*
*the marriage. He made the following findings about Whitney's sex factors,*
*which he divided into six categories: (1) chromosomes (male); (2) gonads*
*(male); (3) genitalia, including internal sex organs (ambiguous); (4) psy-*
*chological factors (female); (5) hormones (no response to testosterone); and*
*(6) secondary sexual characteristics (mixed but primarily female). Based on*
*Whitney's history of self identifying as a female at a young age and choosing*
*to live as a female before her surgery and the diagnosis of PAIS, the court*
*determined that assigning her to the male sex on her birth record was an*
*error. Finally, the court found that she was able to consummate her mar-*
*riage. The judge also placed particular weight on three facts: Whitney had*
*PAIS and PAIS infants currently are typically raised as girls; her genitalia at*
*birth were ambiguous; and from a very early age, Whitney decided to live*
*as female.*[3]

The court's determination that Whitney was a female and that her marriage to a man was a legal heterosexual marriage is far superior to the Australian judge's declaration that Dennis was neither a man nor a woman. The
decision, however, should not be hailed as a model for future courts to follow. To obtain confirmation of her legal status as a female and the validity
of her marriage to William, Whitney was required to provide embarrassing
intimate information about the appearance of her genitalia, her ability to

engage in intercourse, and her preferred position for urinating. Why was she required to answer questions in a public courtroom that most people would believe are too intimate to share with a close friend? Why would someone who had always identified as a female and who had lived her entire adult life as a woman have to agree to subject her body and psyche to such intense scrutiny to attain a status that is automatically bestowed on any person who had an "F" placed on her birth certificate when she was born? Why does the state believe that it needs to carefully police the right of a person with an intersex condition to be treated legally as a man or a woman?

The answer to these questions is not controlled by the government's concern about the sex status of people with intersex conditions. Instead, it is driven by society's perceived need to police the binary sex and gender divide and to prevent the inadvertent sanctioning of same-sex marriages. Courts believe they need to delineate carefully the factors that legally differentiate men from women so that their decisions cannot be used (1) by sex and gender nonconformists to use the law to break down sex and gender stereotypes and (2) by gays and lesbians to open the door to same-sex marriage. State policing of sex and gender identities is discussed in chapter 5. This chapter focuses on courts' concerns about opening the door to marriages of gay and lesbian couples.[4]

During the past two decades, hundreds of articles and books have been written persuasively arguing that laws that limit marriage to heterosexual couples violate the U.S. Constitution and many state constitutions. Successful lobbying efforts and effective court challenges in a number of jurisdictions have opened the marital door to same-sex couples. More than a dozen jurisdictions now allow same-sex couples to wed.[5]

Although the ideal solution would be to eliminate the "opposite-sex" marriage requirement, most jurisdictions still limit marriage to a couple consisting of one man and one woman. Therefore, judges who want to prohibit same-sex marriages carefully police marriage cases involving a transsexual spouse or a spouse with an intersex condition. These courts are concerned that their rulings in these cases could be used by gay and lesbian couples to open the door to same-sex marriage.

A full discussion of the rationales courts use to justify the ban on same-sex marriage is beyond the scope of this book, but a basic understanding of the justifications for limiting marriage to heterosexual unions is necessary to understand the courts' approaches in marriage cases involving a spouse with an intersex condition or who is transsexual. Four major reasons have been advanced in defense of the ban on same-sex marriages: (1) one of the primary purposes of marriage is procreative and same-sex couples cannot procreate; (2) same-sex marriages pose a risk to children because they threaten moral values and because children of same-sex couples would be raised in less than an "ideal" household arrangement containing a mother and a father; (3) marriage, by history and tradition, has always been defined as a union of a man and a woman and allowing same-sex couples to marry violates the traditions and morals of society; and (4) changing the definition of marriage will have far-reaching negative effects because marriage is the foundation on which society has been built and putting same-sex relationships on the same level as traditional marriages would undermine the status that is necessary to preserve traditional marriage.[6]

Although some opponents of same-sex marriage continue to insist that the ability to procreate is a justification for banning same-sex marriage, thousands of couples who are unable to procreate or who choose not to have children are granted marriage licenses without any inquiry into their reproductive capacity. Most of the recent cases challenging this requirement have held that procreative ability is not a prerequisite for heterosexual couples to marry and that it therefore cannot be the basis for denying same-sex couples the right to wed.[7] Many people with an intersex condition are infertile and transsexuals who have undergone hormonal and surgical treatments are usually not able to procreate. Just as infertility does not bar men and women from entering into traditional marriages, it cannot be used to justify any limitation on the marriage rights of gays, lesbians, transsexuals, and people with an intersex condition.

Current reliable studies do not support the argument that household arrangements involving something other than one mother and one father provide less than an "ideal" environment for raising children.[8] Even if future investigations prove that the optimal environment for raising children is in a household with one mother and one father, states do not currently bar single people from raising children. In addition, given the current divorce rate of heterosexual couples, the government sanctions the rearing of a significant percentage of children in households that do not include a traditional mother and father.

Neither infertile heterosexuals nor unmarried people are prohibited from becoming parents based on their procreative incapacity or marital status. Thus, the underlying rationale for limiting the ability of people with an intersex condition and transsexuals to marry in their self-identified gender role is society's perceived need to maintain marriage as a heterosexual institution.

If people with an intersex condition and transsexuals did not seek marriage licenses, states could easily maintain the heterosexual marriage boundary and limit entry to couples consisting of one man and one woman. The sex credentials required would be clear: a marriage would be valid as long as at birth one of the parties was identified as a male and the other was identified as a female. Marriages between people with the same sex indicated on their birth records would be invalid. Transsexuals and persons with an intersex condition whose gender identity do not match the sex indicated at birth challenge the meaning of regulations limiting marriage to one man and one woman.

The perceived importance of limiting marriages to heterosexual unions is best illustrated by the Gender Recognition Act passed by the British Parliament in 2004. The Gender Recognition Act amended British law to greatly ease the ability of transsexuals to be legally recognized as their self-identified gender for all purposes. The law is problematic, however, for married people who want to transition. Consider a couple in which one of the spouses is a male and one is a female. They have been married for years and the male decides to transition to female. Although the couple is in love and wants to remain married, Britain presents them with a Hobson's choice. The transsexual spouse can live as a woman and be legally recognized as a woman only if she first obtains a divorce from her wife. If she wants to stay married, she is not allowed to be legally recognized as a woman. In other words, Britain has adopted a law that promotes the divorce of a happily married couple who may have children.[9]

When a court is asked to decide whether a person can legally marry in a sex role other than the one indicated on the original birth record, the line between a heterosexual and same-sex marriage begins to blur. In the absence of controlling legislation, courts feel obliged to establish the criteria for determining the sex role in which a person can marry. Those who believe that opening marriage to same-sex couples will undermine the basic foundations of our society vigilantly police the sex borders and propose firm criteria for determining a person's sex. Because people with an intersex condition and transsexuals challenge some long-held beliefs about sex and gender, establishing the criteria for determining a person's sex for purposes of marriage becomes problematic for traditional courts. Courts that have been asked to adjudicate marriage cases in which one of the parties has an intersex condition or is a transsexual have failed to develop coherent and consistent standards for determining what makes a man a man and a woman a woman.

Thus far, only two appellate courts have been asked to determine the validity of a marriage in which one of the parties was born with an intersex condition. The Australian Family Court ruled in 1979 that an intersex husband (Dennis in the introductory story at the beginning of this chapter) was neither a man nor a woman and implied that he could not legally marry anyone. Later Australian courts have criticized this result.

The only other case involving a marriage in which one of the parties was born with an intersex condition was decided in England in 2000. In *W v. W*[10] (Whitney in the second story at the beginning of this chapter), the court relied on multiple factors to determine the legal sex of a wife with an intersex condition. The court required twenty-four pages of analysis to reach the conclusion that the male assignment at birth was an error and that W should be considered a woman. The court did not establish a clear-cut test for determining sex. Instead, it relied on a number of factors to reach its conclusion. W's biologic sex markers were an important part of the judge's determination. But W's sex features were a mixture of male and female so they could not be the sole determinant of W's sex. The exact nature of her sexual attributes was so critical to the court's ultimate decision that the court was unwilling simply to accept the medical expert's opinion that W's sex factors were ambiguous. Instead, the court also required W to testify about the appearance of her phallus, gonads, urethra, and vagina. Although W's sex markers could not clearly establish W's legal sex, the court concluded that W could qualify as a legal wife because W had identified as a female from a very early age, other people with W's intersex condition are typically raised as girls, and W could consummate the marriage in the female role.

Although the court wrote an extensive opinion, the decision does not set forth a definitive method for determining a person's legal sex. Instead of establishing a clear "sex test," the court listed the factors that influenced its decision. No single reason was dispositive and the weight given each factor was unclear. Although the court relied on biologic sex attributes, self-identity, and the ability to consummate the marriage, the opinion does not explain why it relied on these factors or which of the reasons it stated was critical. Thus, the court avoided providing a test that could be used by transsexuals or gays and lesbians.

Although many more courts have adjudicated the validity of marriages in which one of the parties was a transsexual, these decisions also fail to establish a clear sex test. Courts have relied on inconsistent factors, creating an intriguing kaleidoscope of contradictory approaches for determining the legal sex of a transsexual. These cases involving a transsexual spouse will likely be relied on as more courts are asked to determine the legal sex of a person with an intersex condition.

England was the first jurisdiction to rule on the issue of sex determination for purposes of marriage. In the 1970 case of *Corbett v. Corbett*,[11] April married a male. Fourteen days after they married, the husband filed for a declaration that the marriage was void because it was an invalid same-sex marriage. The husband alleged that April was born a man and should be legally considered a man for purposes of determining the validity of the marriage.

April asserted that she was born with an intersex condition. The court engaged in a lengthy and in-depth analysis of the medical and psychological aspects of transsexualism and intersexuality. Although the court acknowledged that medical professionals use many factors to determine the appropriate sex in which an individual should live, the court used only three factors to determine a person's sex for the purposes of marriage: chromosomes, gonads, and genitalia. According to the *Corbett* court, chromosomal pattern, gonadal sex, and genitalia define an individual's "true sex." The court determined that April was a male-to-female transsexual, who had male chromosomes (XY) at birth and at the time of the trial, and male gonads (testicles) and genitals (penis) at birth. Therefore, the court ruled that she was still legally a male for purposes of determining whether her marriage to a man was legal. The court opined that an individual's biological sex was assigned at birth and, barring an error, could not later be changed either medically or surgically.

After this decision, most courts followed *Corbett* and decided that for purposes of marriage, transsexuals remain the sex they were assigned at birth. During the next twenty-five years, courts in New York,[12] Ohio,[13] Canada,[14] Singapore,[15] and South Africa[16] ruled that postoperative transsexuals are legally the sex listed on their original birth certificate. In addition, the European Court of Human Rights held that a country's failure to allow postoperative transsexuals to marry in their self-identified gender role did not violate the Convention for the Protection of Human Rights and Fundamental Freedoms.[17]

Before the 1990s, New Jersey was the only court to specifically reject the *Corbett* test. In 1976, in *M.T. v. J.T.*,[18] the New Jersey appellate court conducted an in-depth analysis of how to determine an individual's sex for purposes of marriage. The court ruled that the postoperative male-to-female wife was a woman for purposes of determining the validity of the marriage. The New Jersey court acknowledged that several criteria might be relevant in determining an individual's sex. It also declared that in most instances external genitalia should be the most significant determinant of sex classification at birth. The court decided that the most humane and accurate test for "true sex" for purposes of marriage would be to analyze both anatomy and gender identity. If the genitalia conform to a person's gender identity, psyche, or psychological sex, then that will be the true sex for purposes of marriage.[19]

Beginning in the 1990s, other courts began to adopt similar approaches. In *Attorney General v. Otahuhu Family Court*,[20] the High Court of Wellington in New Zealand ruled that postoperative transsexuals acquire their postoperative sex for purposes of marriage. The court recognized that marital law in New Zealand shifted away from focusing on sexual activity and now placed more emphasis on the psychological and social aspects of sex. The court criticized the *Corbett* decision for its emphasis on chromosomes, genitalia, and gonads as well as for its failure to recognize the overriding importance of social and psychological factors.[21]

Since 2000, courts that have been asked to determine a person's legal sex for purposes of marriage have adopted a variety of approaches. Most courts outside of the United States have rejected the outdated tests used in earlier judicial decisions and have focused on the scientific literature and the importance of hormonal and other influences on the development of gender identity. A number of lower courts in the United States have also followed this approach, but many of these cases have been reversed on appeal.

In 2002, the European Court of Human Rights specifically rejected its earlier decisions that had relied on an outdated understanding of gender identity formation.[22] Beginning in the late 1980s, transsexuals had asked the European Court of Human Rights to rule that their countries' denial of their right to marry in their self-identified gender role violated articles 8 and 12 of the European Convention on Human Rights. Article 8 of the convention protects the right to respect for private life and article 12 protects the right to marry and form a family. For years, the European Court of Human Rights had ruled that countries had the right to deny transsexuals the ability to marry in their self identified gender role.[23] In 2002, the European Court of Human Rights reexamined and rejected its earlier rulings. The court held that refusing to allow transsexuals to marry in their self identified gender role violates the right to privacy under article 8 and the ability to marry under article 12 of the Convention on Human Rights.[24] The court ruled that transsexuals have the right to legal recognition of their self identified sex. Two years later, the British Parliament adopted legislation that treats transsexuals as their self identified sex for all purposes.[25]

Similarly, in 2003, Australia specifically rejected the approach it had taken in its earlier decision. In determining that a female-to-male transsexual was a male for purposes of marriage, Australia held that the plain meaning of the word *male* includes a postoperative female-to-male transsexual. Given the recent scientific evidence on gender identity formation, the court concluded that the fact that a person's eventual sexual identity "cannot be physically determined at birth seems to us to present a strong argument . . . that any determination at that stage is not and should not be immutable."[26]

Developments in the courts in the United States have generally followed the opposite path of the courts of other countries. During the past decade, the issue of the validity of a marriage in which one of the spouses is a transsexual has been litigated in courts in California, Florida, Kansas, Ohio, Illinois, and Texas and by the Board of Immigration Appeals (BIA). Five courts—the California,[27] Louisiana,[28] and Florida[29] trial courts, the Kansas Court of Appeals,[30] and the BIA[31]—held that postoperative transsexuals acquire their self-identified sex as their legal sex. The BIA, Louisiana, and California trial court decisions were not appealed and are still valid, but the Kansas and Florida cases were reversed on appeal. The Supreme Court of Kansas,[32] the Court of Appeals of Florida,[33] the Court of Appeals of Texas,[34] and the Court of Appeals of Ohio[35] all ruled that for purposes of marriage, transsexuals remain forever the sex that was assigned to them at birth.

The reasoning of the U.S. courts that allowed transsexuals to marry in their self-identified gender role is very similar to the approaches taken in the decisions in other countries. In lengthy opinions, the Florida trial court, the Kansas Court of Appeals, and the BIA conducted a thorough review of the medical and legal literature on transsexualism. These courts rejected earlier sex determination decisions that followed *Corbett* as "a rigid and simplistic approach to issues that are far more complex than addressed."[36]

Courts that continued to follow *Corbett* did so for a number of reasons. They relied on the plain meaning rule, religious rhetoric, or a desire to defer to the legislature.

A number of courts have relied on general rules of statutory construction, and in particular the plain meaning rule, to determine the legislative intent behind statutes that limit marriage to one man and one woman. The plain meaning rule requires courts to interpret statutory terms in accordance with their ordinary meaning unless the statute provides a different definition. Although courts have relied on the plain meaning rule to determine who is a man and who is a woman, such reliance has led to contradictory results. For example, the Australian Court of Appeals and the Florida trial court believed that the plain and ordinary meaning of the word *male* encompassed a post-operative female-to-male transsexual. In contrast, appellate courts in Ohio,[37] Kansas,[38] and Florida[39] found that the plain meaning of the terms *male* and *female* could be found in the dictionary. The Kansas Supreme Court allowed an estranged son to inherit his father's multimillion-dollar estate by claiming his stepmother was not legally a woman who could marry a man. To determine her legal sex, the court quoted *Webster's* dictionary and determined that *male* is defined as "designating or of the sex that fertilizes the ovum and begets offspring: opposed to female." *Female* is defined as "designating or of the sex that produces ova and bears offspring: Opposed to male."[40] The Florida and Ohio courts approved of this approach. In other words, the Kansas, Ohio, and Florida courts have implied that those who cannot fertilize and beget are not true men and those who cannot produce ova and bear offspring are not true women. These definitions may come as a shock to the millions of people who cannot bear or beget offspring. The estimated number of infertile adult women in the United States is 6.1 million, about 10 percent of the reproductive age population.[41]

Some judges also rejected scientific literature and instead relied on religious rhetoric to support their decision. For example, the Texas Court of Appeals allowed a physician to escape paying damages to the transsexual wife of a man who had died as a result of the doctor's malpractice. The court recognized that sex determination involves profound philosophical, metaphysical, and policy concerns. Despite these profound concerns, the court decided that when "our Creator" creates transsexuals, "our Creator" intends for them to remain the sex they are labeled at birth. The court phrased the legal question this way: "The deeper philosophical (and now legal) question is: can a physician change the gender of a person with a scalpel, drugs and counseling, or is a person's gender immutably fixed by our Creator at birth?"[42]

Finally, the recent decisions in which courts refused to allow transsexuals to adopt their postoperative sex found that they did not have the power to determine the test for legal sex in the face of legislative inaction.[43] Although the legislative histories in these jurisdictions indicate the legislatures had not considered the issue of sex determination for transsexuals, these courts decided that legislative silence is equivalent to legislative disapproval.

In addition to these cases involving postoperative transsexuals, a court in Illinois ruled that a female-to-male transsexual who had not undergone a vaginectomy, reduction mammoplasty, metoidioplasty, scrotoplasty, urethroplasty, and phalloplasty could not be considered a male for purposes of marriage. This court refused to recognize his amended birth certificate that indicated he was a male because it found that the mere issuance of a new birth certificate is not conclusive proof that a person has changed legal sex for purposes of marriage. The court did not rule out the possibility that he could eventually become a legal male; it held that he had not yet undergone the procedures that would qualify him as a male.[44]

The recent marriage validity cases involving a transsexual spouse fall into two categories: those that have concluded that a person's legal sex for purposes of marriage is fixed at birth and those that examine the physical and psychological sex attributes as they exist at the time of the marriage. Courts in the first category have created bright-line sex determination tests that have the effect of ensuring that transsexuals, gays, and lesbians cannot inadvertently attain the right to marry. These courts have refused to acknowledge that gender self-identity is not controlled by chromosomes, gonads, and genitalia. They have ignored an extensive body of scientific literature that indicates that gender identity formation is a complex process that is not yet fully understood. By ruling that legal sex for purposes of marriage is fixed by the sex assigned at birth, these courts believe that they are ensuring that marriage remains a heterosexual institution.

Ironically, by denying transsexuals the ability to marry in their self-identified sex role, courts are actually sanctioning what to all outward appearances are same-sex marriages. Although society tends to conflate the concepts of gender identity and sexual orientation, they are in fact unrelated. A male-to-female transsexual may be sexually attracted to another woman and a female-to-male transsexual may be sexually attracted to another man. Therefore, courts that have ruled that legal sex is fixed at birth are sanctioning marriages between two people that society would perceive as the same sex.[45]

Although no marriage case in the United States has involved a spouse with an intersex condition, the rules developed in the cases involving a transsexual spouse will likely affect the outcome when a case involving a spouse with an intersex condition is eventually litigated. Such a case is being considered by the Texas attorney general.

*Virgil Eugene Hill was born in New York. At the time of Hill's birth, the doctors proclaimed that the baby was a boy and an "M" was placed on the New York birth certificate. Although Hill lived as a male and served in the Vietnam War, Hill never felt comfortable with the male designation. At the age of twenty-eight, during a medical examination, doctors discovered that Hill had ovaries. Hill opted to undergo surgery to feminize her body and she legally changed her name to Sabrina in 1991.*

*In 2010, Sabrina wanted to marry her longtime partner, Therese "Tee" Bur. They were denied a marriage license in El Paso, Texas. The El Paso county attorney, Jo Anne Bernal, claimed that she was unclear whether Sabrina was legally a male, as indicated on her New York birth certificate, or legally a female, as indicated on her Texas driver's license and a name change order issued by a Washington State court. Bernal asked the Texas attorney general, Greg Abbott, for a ruling.*

*In the meantime, Sabrina and Tee decided to marry instead in San Antonio, which is located in Bexar County, Texas. Bexar County issued the marriage license, relying on the male indication on Sabrina's birth certificate. The Bexar County clerk, Gerard C. Rickhoff, decided that the controlling ruling was* Littleton, *in which a Texas court of appeals declared a marriage between Jonathon, a male, and Christie Lee Littleton, a male-to-female transsexual, an invalid same-sex marriage. The* Littleton *court declared that Christie was still legally a man because she had XY chromosomes and an "M" on her original birth certificate. Based on* Littleton, *Bexar County has allowed couples who outwardly appear to be the same sex to marry, as long as their birth records indicate that one was born a male and one was born a female.*

*Bernal is still seeking a clarifying ruling from the attorney general's office regarding which documents should be used to establish a person's legal sex for purposes of marriage. Texas amended its laws in 2009 to allow nineteen different documents to be used to prove age and identity when parties seek a marriage license. The law does not indicate the appropriate outcome if the sex indicator on the documents is not consistent. Hill submitted three documents, two of which had a female indicator and one of which, the original birth certificate, indicated she was a male. Thus far, the Texas attorney general has not issued an opinion, so the validity of marriages in Texas involving persons with an intersex condition is unclear.*[46]

As long as same-sex marriages are banned, courts will continue to be in the business of establishing a person's legal sex for purposes of marriage. In addition, this issue may be resolved by legislation. For example, in 2007 in California, Protect Marriage and Vote Yes Marriage, two organizations that oppose same-sex marriages, proposed a number of ballot initiatives that would have amended the California Constitution. One of the proposals, called "The Voter's Right to Protect Marriage," defined the terms *male* and *female*. The initiative's definitions stated, "a man is an adult male human being who possesses at least one inherited Y chromosome, and a woman is an adult female human being who does not possess an inherited Y chromosome." This initiative was not included on the ballot, but similar proposals could be considered.[47] Applying this definition to a number of people with an intersex condition would lead to absurd results. For example, women with complete androgen insensitivity syndrome have an X and a Y chromosome. Therefore, in utero, their gonads develop into testicles, which remain nestled in their abdominal cavity. Because their body receptors are unable to read the testosterone produced by the testicles, they develop female bodies and a female gender identity. Under the proposed legislation, these women who have a female phenotype, female genitalia, and a female gender identity would be defined as male and only allowed to marry another woman because of their Y chromosome. Most people would consider this union to be a same-sex marriage.

Courts that have ruled that people are limited to marrying in the sex role assigned to them at birth have believed that such rulings promote traditional morals and values. When these courts are presented with a marriage involving a person with an intersex condition or a transsexual who also identifies as gay or lesbian, they will need to reassess exactly what values their earlier rulings have furthered.

# 5

# What's in a Name?

Katherine Marie McIntyre is fifty-one years old and has been living openly as a woman for more than five years. She dresses as a woman and holds herself out to be a woman. Her apartment lease, bank accounts, credit card accounts, and club memberships are all under the name Katherine Marie. She has been taking female hormones for seven years to feminize her body. The only location where she is addressed as Robert and treated as a man is at her job with the Harrisburg Parking Authority, where she has worked for more than ten years. Her employer refuses to call her anything other than Robert, unless she has her name legally changed.

When Katherine petitioned a Pennsylvania court for a legal change of name, a board certified medical physician with a specialty in psychiatry testified as an expert witness. Dr. Thornsby recommended a name change so that Katherine could live her life fully as a woman. Despite this medical testimony, the court refused to grant Katherine's petition to change her name until she could prove that she has completed "sex reassignment" surgery. For Katherine to be entitled to use a female name, the court required her to undergo the "irreversible" step of surgical alteration that would modify her outward anatomy to render her a female. The court held that to allow a name change from an obviously male name to an obviously female name prior to sex reassignment surgery would be to sanction the perpetration of a deception on the public.

In denying Katherine's petition, the court relied on its strong interest in avoiding negative consequences to the public. It stated that it was concerned about census statistics and the need for providers of sanitation facilities to have a clear-cut, decisive, well-accepted indicator of gender to facilitate the health, sanitary, and comfort needs of the public. The court asserted that approving a name change for a person who had not undergone irreversible surgery would attach legal validity to what is at best a "half truth" and would aid in the perpetration of a deceit on society. It believed that society can only function if it can rely on the courts to draw fixed and meaningful distinctions.

The court stated, "A rose is a rose. Remove one petal and it is still a rose. It is unnecessary to probe into the intricacies of biology and the absoluteness of genetic identity. But, one can go so far as to agree that at the point where one has removed every single petal from a rose, only then is it reasonable to say that it is a stem. Therefore, for these purposes here, in the same way that the complete and irreversible act of removing all of the petals from a 'rose' renders it a 'stem' and no longer a 'rose,' this court holds that the complete and irreversible act of sex reassignment surgery will legally change the person of Robert Henry McIntyre into Katherine Marie McIntyre."[1]

This court's questionable metaphor illustrates the view of many courts that deny people the ability to amend their official documents to reflect their name and self-identified gender. Many judges tend to view males and females as opposite poles of a binary divide that must be carefully policed. They are unwilling to allow people to cross that boundary unless they present irrefutable and irreversible evidence that they can never return to live as their original sex.

This approach is not universal. For example, in 2004, Great Britain dramatically eased the standards required to obtain a Gender Recognition Certificate that recognizes a transsexual's transition into the other sex.[2] Australia and India have gone one step further. Australia will allow the use of a sex marker other than the binary male/female indicators on its citizens' passports. Australia has allowed the sex marker to indicate "X," meaning that the person is either indeterminate sex or intersex.[3] In 2009, India began to allow transsexuals and people with an intersex condition to mark "O," for other, as the gender on voter registration forms.[4]

Rulings that force people to carry official documents that do not accurately reflect their self-identified gender and appearance can dramatically disrupt people's lives. Many official documents, including birth certificates, passports, and driver's licenses, indicate an individual's name and sex. These documents are used for a variety of purposes including security clearances, proof of identity in financial transactions, and proof of citizenship when crossing borders or applying for a job. Carrying documents that do not match the apparent sex of the holder could lead to embarrassment, denial of benefits, and other more severe consequences, such as detainment and incarceration.

This chapter examines the statutes and court decisions that affect people's ability to change the name and sex designation on their original birth certificate and other official documents, including passports, Social Security records, and driver's licenses. It also explains and critiques the reasons government agents have used to force people to carry official documents that do not accurately reflect their self-identified name and gender. The legal rules controlling the ability to modify the gender marker on a person's official documents have a clear impact on transsexuals. People with an intersex condition may be subjected to these same barriers if they do not develop a gender self-identity that matches the sex assigned to them at birth.

## Statutes and Administrative Agency Rules Addressing Sex Amendments

### Birth Certificates

Because the birth certificate is the first official document to indicate sex, it usually controls the sex designation on all later documents. As discussed in chapter 1, sex on a birth certificate is usually established by the medical attendant assisting at the birth. The presence of an "adequate" penis typically leads to the label *male*, and the absence of an "adequate" penis leads to the label *female*. If the external genitalia are ambiguous, medical officials will typically recommend that the genitalia be modified so that they have a clearly male or female appearance. Then, the official sex indicated on the certificate will match the appearance of the genitalia.

If an error is made on the original certificate, governmental agencies will typically issue a new or amended certificate. In contrast, changes in the birth certificate for a later "change of sex" are not as easily obtained. Acquiring an amended certificate may be difficult even in the case of a mistaken identification at birth. For example, it took parents approximately a decade and required the intervention of Princess Diana to convince the Office of National Statistics in Great Britain to issue a new birth certificate to a girl born with an intersex condition.

*Joella was born with a rare intersex condition. The infant's genitalia were not clearly male or female. In addition, the bladder and intestines were outside her body and she had a large opening in her abdominal wall. Her condition was so serious that doctors advised the parents that the baby would be unlikely to survive. The parents hastened to christen the newborn. Her mother had not thought of any girl's names, so they christened her Joel David. Despite the odds against her, the baby survived an eight-hour surgery and she recently celebrated her eighteenth birthday.*

*After it was apparent that the baby would survive, the parents consulted medical experts about the appropriate gender for raising their child. Based*

*on the doctors' advice, the parents decided to raise her as a girl. The par-
ents renamed her Joella and they tried to amend her birth records to reflect
the correct name and gender designation. Government officials refused to
amend the birth record. After years of fighting with government agents,
Joella's story made international headlines. Finally, when Joella was approximately ten years old, aided by an intervention by Princess Diana, the parents
were able to convince the Office of National Statistics to change Joella's birth
certificate to indicate that her sex was female.[5]*

Joella's story is the only public report about a person with an intersex
condition encountering problems amending the sex designator on official
records. Transsexuals are much more commonly denied this right, but anecdotal evidence indicates that adults and minors with an intersex condition
who seek to change their gender marker may be encountering increased
resistance.[6] Although the remaining discussion in this chapter focuses primarily on the ability of transsexuals to amend their official documents,
people with an intersex condition may eventually face the same problems
encountered by transsexuals.

In the United States, most jurisdictions allow transsexuals to amend their
birth certificates. Thirty-five states and the District of Columbia have adopted
statutes or administrative regulations that specifically address the ability of
people who undergo sex transition procedures to amend the sex designation
on their birth certificate.[7] These jurisdictions do not all require the same type
of proof to be entitled to an amendment. Most require a court order, but some
will amend the birth certificate based on a certified medical letter from a treating physician asserting that the person's sex has been surgically changed.[8]

In addition to the jurisdictions with specific legislation addressing sex redes-
ignations sought by transsexuals, fourteen states allow general amendments to
the birth record.[9] Of these jurisdictions, eleven states will issue an amended
birth certificate indicating a change in sex.[10] Two states, Idaho and Ohio, do not
allow these amendments and the rule in Texas is unclear. In Idaho, the Office
of Vital Statistics has refused to issue amended birth certificates reflecting a
change of sex.[11] In Ohio, a probate court ruled that the general birth certificate
amendment statute does not apply to amendments sought by individuals who
have undergone surgical procedures to change their sex.[12] Texas used to allow
an amendment to a birth certificate based on a sex change, but it is questionable
whether Texas still allows such amendments.[13] The only state with a statute specifically prohibiting a sex change on the birth record is Tennessee.[14]

In sum, thirty-five U.S. jurisdictions (thirty-four states plus the District of Columbia) have adopted statutes or administrative rulings specifically authorizing a legal sex change on the birth certificate. Eleven additional states permit such amendments under their general birth certificate amendment statutes or administrative agency policies. Three states that authorize general amendments to birth records refuse to grant amendments to the sex indicated. One state has adopted a statute specifically banning a legal change of sex on birth certificates.

## Federal Documentation: Social Security Records and Passports

The sex marker on the birth certificate typically controls the sex that will be included on Social Security records and passports. The Social Security Administration and the State Department both allow amendments to the sex designated on their records. An amendment to a Social Security record requires proof of genital surgery.[15] Until 2010, the State Department only allowed transsexuals to amend the sex marker on their passport if the applicant provided proof of completed genital surgery. The State Department would issue a temporary one-year passport to transsexuals who had not yet completed surgery.[16]

In 2010, the State Department amended its requirements to reflect the standards and recommendations of the World Professional Association for Transgender Health (WPATH), which the American Medical Association recognizes as the authority in this field. Beginning on June 10, 2010, to receive an amended passport, transsexuals need only present a certificate from a medical physician stating that the applicant has undergone appropriate clinical treatment for gender transition. The 2010 standards state that sex reassignment surgery is not a prerequisite for changing the gender marker and that such documentation should not be requested by government officials.[17]

For the first time, the State Department also addressed the ability of people with an intersex condition to amend their gender marker on their passport. The new rules allow people with an intersex condition to amend the sex designation on their passports based on a statement from a licensed physician who has treated the person and evaluated the gender-related medical history.[18]

## Driver's Licenses

Many jurisdictions will more easily allow a change to the sex indicator on the driver's license than on the birth certificate. According to a survey of motor vehicle bureaus, all states and the District of Columbia indicated that they would issue new licenses with new sex indicators to postoperative transsexuals. Fifteen states and the District of Columbia do not require the completion of gender changing surgery and will change the sex indicator based on a letter from the treating physician that states that the person is in the process of gender change. The remaining states require surgery.[19]

As this discussion indicates, a number of government agencies deal with documents in which a gender marker appears. Many people have at least four documents indicating their sex—a birth certificate, a driver's license, a passport, and a Social Security record. Each agency creates its own rules controlling name and sex change amendments. Therefore, a person with an intersex condition and transsexuals who seek to amend all their official records may end up with some of their records indicating they are female and other records indicating they are male.

## Court Decisions Addressing Requests for an Amendment

Although the legislative trend is to allow amendments to the sex designation on federal and state documents, some courts have refused to allow revisions to the birth record without a specific statute authorizing the change. The reasons these courts have advanced to justify their rulings include (1) prevention of fraud;[20] (2) fear that the document could be used to establish one's legal sex for other purposes, such as marriage;[21] (3) a belief that the legal system should not be used to "help psychologically ill persons" in their social adaptation;[22] and (4) a belief that birth certificates are historical records that should accurately reflect the true facts as they existed at the time of the birth.[23] None of these policy concerns justifies use of the sex indicated at birth as the "official sex" for all legal documents or a requirement of surgical alteration to obtain an amendment.

The first justification, prevention of fraud, can be accomplished most effectively by using a person's self-identified sex. If a person presents as a female, her official documents should accurately reflect how she appears. Clearly, a person's gonads, chromosomes, and genitalia are not inspected to determine identity when one is stopped at an international border or by a traffic officer. Physical appearance, which is generally a reflection of self-identified sex, is the fact that should match the sex indicated on the official document.

The second justification, that allowing self-identification on a person's official documents will lead to gay and lesbian marriages, can be addressed by legislatures adopting appropriate limiting language if they choose to do so.[24] Moreover, the current laws in some states already lead to this result. Ironically, in jurisdictions that refuse to recognize a person's self-identified sex for matrimonial purposes, male-to-female transsexuals have entered into legal marriages with another female. In other words, some jurisdictions that ban same-sex marriage allow two individuals whose gender identity, physical appearance, and genitalia are female to marry each other.[25]

The third justification, not assisting "psychologically ill people," clearly does not apply to people with an intersex condition. These individuals are not confused about their sexual identity because of a psychological problem; they have biological sex aspects that are not all clearly male or female. Furthermore, using this argument to prevent transsexuals from amending the sex and name indicators on their official documents is not justifiable. Psychological research about transsexuals indicates that transsexualism may have a biological basis and cannot be "cured" or "corrected" by therapy. A court's refusal to allow amendments to birth certificates will not deter transsexuals from living their lives in their self-identified sex. Given the ostracism that they suffer at the hands of society before they choose to adopt a new identity, the legal barriers are minor. Most important, courts that refuse to allow a name or sex marker change are assuming that transsexualism is a disease, rather than simply a variation in gender identity. Transsexuals are not "psychologically ill" because they do not fit societal norms of gender identity.[26]

The final justification, maintaining the birth certificate as a historical record, is clearly not an accurate reflection of the legislative intent. Typically, amendments to birth certificates are made following an adoption, change of name for minors, and acknowledgment of paternity. If legislatures allow amendments in these circumstances, legislators do not intend that the birth certificate should reflect only accurate historical facts that were true at the time of birth. Furthermore, in the case of people with an intersex condition who were misidentified at birth, the sex indicator established at birth is inaccurate.

The rules that limit people's right to have their official sex markers reflect their self-identified sex are ineffective at meeting the legislative goals. Forcing people who appear to be females to carry male identity cards will likely result in embarrassment, ridicule, and harassment and may lead to violent assault and arrest. Self-identification should be the determining sex factor. Official documents are usually reviewed to make sure that the person presents as the person indicated on the documents. Height, weight, eye color, and general physical appearance—not genitalia, gonads, and chromosomes—are reviewed to make sure these descriptors match the person using the official document.

The development of our understanding about how gender identity and sexual orientation are formed is in its infancy. The millions of people whose biological markers are not all clearly male or female and the thousands of people whose gender identity does not match their biological markers illustrate that gender is not always clear or necessarily binary and fixed. Contrary to the assertion of the Pennsylvania court quoted in the introduction to this chapter, humans are not always flourishing roses or barren stems. Determining the sex that should be reflected on a person's official documents should not be based on such an inapt metaphor.

# 6

# Where May I Live and
# Which Bathroom Do I Use?

*"S, a postoperative male-to-female transsexual, started to use the women's restroom at the law school she was attending."*

*"There was an enormous outcry from women students of all political persuasions, who 'felt raped,' in addition to the more academic assertions of some who 'feared rape.' In a complicated storm of homophobia, the men of the student body let it be known that they too 'feared rape' and vowed to chase her out of any and all men's rooms. The oppositional forces of men and women reached a compromise: S should use the dean's bathroom. Alas, in the dean's bathroom no resolution was found, for the suggestion had not been an honest one but merely an integration of the fears of each side. Then, in his turn the dean, circumspection having gotten him this far in life, expressed polite, well-modulated fears about the appearance of impropriety in having students visit his inner sanctum. . . . At the vortex of this torment, S as human being who needed to go to the bathroom was lost."[1]*

*Jackie Tates wrote a threatening letter to the governor of California. For that crime, California placed her in total isolation in a maximum security prison. Despite her repeated requests to be housed with the general prisoner popula-tion, she was kept in isolation for over a year. She was denied the right to shower, to use the day room, or to visit with a chaplain on a regular basis. She was not allowed to attend church or Bible study, participate in recre-ational activities, or use the library. She had limited access to the day room and cleaning supplies, so she spent most of her time in isolation in a filthy cell. Although she posed no risk to her own or others' physical safety, she was heavily shackled and manacled whenever she was transported outside the jail. Jackie was placed in isolation and treated as a high-risk prisoner solely because she was a transsexual.[2]*

Sex segregated housing and bathroom facilities are accepted as the norm in our society. Although some colleges now allow students to share bathrooms and dormitory rooms with members of a different sex, such arrangements are not typical.³ Most public housing, including college dormitories, prisons, foster care facilities, and homeless shelters, are sex segregated. In addition, although some public venues now provide a gender neutral or family use bathroom, the vast majority of restrooms are limited to use by one sex.

This "natural" division is often used to justify discrimination against people whose bodies do not conform to sex or gender norms. Nontraditional women are consistently denied the right to use women's facilities or to be housed with other women based on the privacy and safety concern of the other women using the facilities. Most of the reported cases banning individuals from public facilities have involved transsexuals because most adult intersex people were subjected to cosmetic genital surgery when they were infants. If the number of these surgeries diminishes, people with an intersex condition are more likely to confront these issues in the future because their genitalia will not clearly fit the female norm.

The previous two chapters address sex determination for purposes of establishing the validity of a marriage and the appropriate sex marker on official documents. As these chapters illustrate, sex determination in these two arenas is not always consistent. Different governmental agencies may use a variety of tests to determine the sex that will appear on various official documents. Furthermore, even if the sex markers on the documents are all congruent, that person may still be denied the ability to marry in the sex role that matches the sex indicated on the official documents.⁴

Sex determination for appropriate housing and bathroom use adds an additional twist to the analysis because of concerns relating to privacy and safety that do not arise in the marriage and official document cases. Reactions to what is viewed as "inappropriate" bathroom use can be extreme. A female member of the Italian Parliament, after finding a male-to-female transsexual member of the Italian Parliament using a female toilet facility, said, "It felt like sexual violence—I really felt ill."⁵ This type of reaction is all too common.

As indicated in this quotation and the stories at the beginning of this chapter, the focus of the discussion in housing and bathroom cases is often on the emotional reaction of the people sharing space with a transsexual. The anguish suffered by those who are denied access to these spaces far surpasses the angst felt by nontranssexuals. Imagine being denied access to public restrooms, being forced to use a man's locker room when you identify as female, or being placed in solitary confinement because you are not allowed to be housed with female prisoners and you will be raped if you are housed in the male population.

Although these decisions have a profound effect on the daily lives of transsexuals and people with an intersex condition, sex determination related to housing, locker room use, and bathroom use in most jurisdictions is typically made on an ad hoc basis by a variety of people. Although some institutions, such as jails and homeless shelters, have written policies, more often than not, decisions are made on the spot by retail clerks, intake personnel, locker room attendants, and sometimes police officers, without reference to written policies.

Most jurisdictions have not adopted specific legislation governing the ability of transsexuals and people with an intersex condition to access facilities appropriate to their gender identity. Even in jurisdictions that prohibit discrimination based on gender identity, some legislatures have specifically exempted bathrooms and locker rooms from these statutes.[6] Moreover, in jurisdictions that do not expressly exclude these spaces, some courts have ruled that these laws are inapplicable to housing, locker room use, and bathroom use.[7]

Although gender determination and segregation issues are critical in college dormitories, foster care facilities, and locker rooms, most of the litigated and reported cases have involved bathroom use and housing in prison. The remainder of this chapter focuses on these two spheres.

## Bathroom Use

Most jurisdictions do not have legislation that addresses discrimination against transsexuals and people with an intersex condition. Even if a jurisdiction prohibits discrimination based on gender identity, transsexuals are often barred from using the restroom appropriate to their gender identity. Courts denying transsexuals access to appropriate bathrooms typically rely on four justifications: (1) a generalized fear about criminal activity, (2) the need to prevent gender fraud, (3) heteronormativity, and (4) the societal need to enforce sex stereotypes.[8]

For example, in *Goins v. West Group*,[9] the Minnesota Human Rights Act (MHRA) prohibited discrimination based on "having or being perceived as having a self-image or identity not traditionally associated with one's biological maleness or femaleness."[10] Julienne Goins was a male-to-female transsexual employed by West Group. She was originally based in New York, where she had been allowed to use the women's restrooms. When she transferred to Minnesota, female co-workers complained about her use of the women's facilities. Her employer told her that she was prohibited from using the women's restrooms. She was told to use one of two single-sex bathrooms that were both far from her work station. One bathroom was actually located in another building. When Julienne complained that these bathrooms were inconveniently located and that they were dirty, her employer refused to change its rule. The company based its decision on the fact that female co-workers were uncomfortable sharing the same bathroom with her. Julienne sued West Group, alleging that she had suffered discrimination under the MHRA. The Minnesota Supreme Court ruled in favor of West Group. It found that the prohibition against discrimination based on gender identity did not extend to traditional sex segregated private spaces, such as locker rooms and restrooms.[11]

In *Hispanic AIDS Forum v. Bruno*,[12] the New York Court of Appeals agreed with the approach adopted in the Minnesota decision. In this case, a landlord refused to renew a lease to a nonprofit organization that offered HIV/AIDS counseling services to the Latino community. The landlord based its decision on the complaints of other building tenants about transsexual clients using the public restrooms. It conditioned the lease renewal on the transsexual clients' limiting their use of the public restrooms. The New York court ruled that no legal violation occurs when transsexual clients are forced to use the restroom that comports with their "biological gender" (the sex assigned to them at birth) rather than their "biological self-image."[13]

One of the few cases in which the effect on the transsexual worker was taken into account was *Cruzan v. Special School District #1*.[14] In *Cruzan*, a female teacher complained when the school permitted the use of the women's restroom by the school librarian, a male-to-female transsexual. In her complaint, the teacher asserted that the school was violating her right to religious freedom and had created a hostile work environment. The court dismissed her lawsuit and upheld the school's decision to allow the transsexual librarian to access the women's restroom.

## Prisoner Housing

*"As a homosexual/transsexual prisoner standing at five foot, four inches tall and weighing under 130 pounds, I find myself at the mercy of other prisoners. Within three months of my arrival at prison, I found myself sexually enslaved by a single domineering prisoner and forced to perform sexual favors in exchange for my "protection" due to the deprivation of reasonable safety.*

*"After requesting Protective Custody asserting claims of prison rape and sexual slavery, I was blatantly denied Protective Custody on repeated occasions and forced from one prison to the other, where I was continuously raped, extorted and sexually assaulted at the hands of other prisoners."*[15]

The violence perpetrated against sex and gender nonconformists that prevails in our society is exacerbated in the prison system. Gender nonconforming prisoners, especially those with a feminine appearance, housed in male prison sections are subjected to severe abuse. Most prison systems do not have written policies addressing how to determine where sex and gender nonconforming prisoners should be housed. Most correctional facilities generally assign prisoners to facilities on the basis of the appearance of their genitalia. Therefore, prisoners with an intersex condition who have ambiguous genitalia or genitalia that do not match their gender identity, as well as transsexuals who have not undergone genital surgery, typically are housed in facilities that do not match their gender self-identity. Housing prisoners with a female identity and ambiguous or male appearing genitalia with male prisoners virtually guarantees that they will be subjected to sexual and other abuse.[16]

At times, sex and gender nonconforming prisoners may be taken out of the general prison population if prison authorities believe their safety is at risk. Prison officials recognize that placing a self-identified female with ambiguous or male genitalia in the male population is dangerous, but they typically will refuse to place her in the female population, even if there is no indication that such a placement would lead to sexual abuse of another female inmate. Most prison facilities do not have separate units for sex and gender nonconformists. Therefore, if officials believe that housing transsexuals or people with an intersex condition in either the male or female population could create problems, officials may separate them from the rest of the prison population and place them in administrative segregation. Although administrative segregation is technically designed to protect the prisoner from harm that would be inflicted in the general population, conditions in segregation units effectively constitute solitary confinement, a system designed to punish prisoners for misbehavior. Prison officials have segregated people with an intersex condition and transsexuals in horrendous conditions, solely because of their intersex or transsexual status.

*Miki Ann DiMarco, a female who was born with an intersex condition, was convicted for check fraud and was placed on probation. When she violated the terms of the probation, she was imprisoned. Despite a security threat rating that indicated that she posed no risk to herself or others, she spent 438 days in solitary confinement in a maximum security prison. She was not allowed to interact with other inmates and she had limited access to the day room, the commissary, educational opportunities, haircuts, religious items, a radio, a lamp, or playing cards. She was forced to eat her meals alone in her cell, while sitting either on her bed or on the toilet. Miki was placed in solitary confinement because she was born with an intersex condition. Despite the fact that she had lived as a female since puberty and was not sexually functional as a male, she remained in isolation throughout her incarceration.[17]*

*Sophia, a male-to-female transsexual in the Florida prison system, had been placed in the protective custody unit supposedly for her protection. While she was in this unit, she was raped. "When he started I yelled Stop, but nobody heard me. When he was done, he left. I closed and locked my door and cried all night." "I believe that for the State to send me to prison for a first-time, non-violent offense is only placing my life in danger. I am not a danger to the public, so why is the State knowingly placing me in danger?"[18]*

A number of prisoners have challenged this abusive system in the courts, alleging that being placed in administrative segregation or being put in the general male population violates their constitutional rights, specifically their right under the Eighth Amendment to be free from cruel and unusual punishment. In *Farmer v. Brennan*, Dee Farmer, a male-to-female transsexual, was beaten and raped by another inmate when she was placed in the general male population. The U.S. Supreme Court held that the prison officials could be held liable for violating Farmer's Eighth Amendment right to be free from cruel and unusual punishment, but only if the prison officials knew that she was being abused by other inmates and acted with deliberate disregard of an excessive risk to her health and safety.[19]

Although prisoners can technically recover damages if they are harmed by being placed in the male population or administrative segregation, significant barriers to recovery exist. Some prisoners lose their cases because they fail to exhaust their administrative remedies before proceeding to court.[20] Exhausting their administrative remedies requires prisoners to report their complaints to prison officials and await their decision. Prisoners often choose not to complain, lest they be labeled a snitch, which is likely to lead to further abuse. In addition, prisoners find it difficult to prove knowledge and deliberate disregard on the part of the prison officials. Finally, courts generally uphold a decision to place prisoners in administrative segregation to protect them from the abuse they would suffer in the general male population. For example, in *Lamb v. Maschner*[21] and *Farmer v. Carlson*,[22] the courts rejected a prisoner's request that she be placed in a female prison. The courts held that segregation in administrative confinement was a reasonable option.

The naturalness of dividing housing and bathroom spaces should not be an axiomatic presumption. Prisons and restrooms have not always been separated by sex. Terry Kogan, in "Sex-Separation in Public Restrooms: Law, Architecture, and Gender,"[23] challenges the genesis and naturalness of the belief that sex segregated facilities constitute a gender neutral policy that merely reflects the anatomical differences between men and women. In a well-developed article, he illustrates how sex-segregated restroom facilities were established in response to nineteenth-century ideology about the appropriate role of women in society. He also examines how the current practices harm a number of people, including people with an intersex condition, transsexuals, people with disabilities requiring assistance from an opposite-sex aide, parents needing to accompany an opposite-sex minor child into the bathroom, and women forced to endure interminable lines at public events while the men's restroom remains open.

Strict enforcement of rules regarding sex-segregated facilities reinforces gender stereotypes that women are vulnerable and men are predators. Although private female spaces may be necessary to protect women from harm, applying these rules to male-to-female transsexuals perpetuates the stereotype that sexual minorities (including gays and transsexuals) are more prone to commit sex crimes. Furthermore, the separation of facilities into "male" and "female" spaces reinforces the view that sex is binary and clear, which leads to additional harm and the further marginalization of transsexuals and people with an intersex condition. As Kogan concludes, "public restrooms have served as a flashpoint in debates over the meaning of gender and gender difference in society. Understanding that sex-separation of this architectural space is not natural or inevitable enables us to envision alternatives."[24]

# PART III

Legal Paths to Enhancing the Lives of
People with an Intersex Condition

# Developing Strategies

As discussed in part I, many people born with an intersex condition have suffered lifelong physical and emotional trauma from traditional medical practices. Creating opportunities to engage in meaningful dialogue among the people most affected (individuals with an intersex condition and their family members) and the people who have the most power to affect decision making (physicians) is critical. In the past decade, progress has been made toward this goal and some doctors are receptive to incorporating the concerns and opinions of some intersex activists. The conversations have been limited, however, and opinions within the medical community still differ widely about how infants born with an intersex condition should be treated. The 2006 Consensus Statement on Management of Intersex Disorders incorporates some of the views of the intersex movement and recognizes the harm inflicted by the gender, sex, and disability presumptions supporting the traditional medical approach. Most physicians, however, have not modified their practices to incorporate the recommendations of the 2006 Consensus Statement.[1] Furthermore, some intersex activists believe that the 2006 Consensus Statement does not go far enough to curtail infant genital surgery.

Anthropologist and bioethicist Katrina Karkazis conducted extensive interviews with medical practitioners and people with an intersex condition and their family members. She concludes that surprisingly little change has occurred in medical practices or the arguments used to justify the procedures. Many surgeons no longer automatically feminize XY infants born with a small phallus or with male genitalia that do not fit the norm. In contrast, cosmetic genital surgeries to "normalize" atypical genitalia to enhance "psychosocial well-being" have not abated to any significant degree. Most surgeons continue to surgically alter genitalia to reinforce the sex assignment, especially in cases in which the eventual gender identity is not clear.[2]

Can legal institutions play a productive role in enhancing the well-being of people born with an intersex condition? Scholars in other disciplines, including medicine, bioethics, history, psychology, sociology, and anthropology, have provided persuasive arguments for modifying the current treatment protocol. Legal advocacy can also play an important role and part III of this book explores the potential for using legal strategies.

Developing legal approaches requires a more in-depth understanding of the goals of the intersex movement. As discussed in chapter 8, intersex activists agree that the primary goal of the movement is to end medical practices that have the potential to cause irreparable physical harm and psychological trauma. In addition, some people in the intersex movement believe that society itself requires transformation. Our society, including our laws and the cultural assumptions on which they are based, support a binary sex and gender system in which heterosexuality is prized over homosexuality and bodily differences are viewed as impairments rather than variations.

This system leads to direct and indirect harm to people with an intersex condition. It may be one of the primary reasons doctors encourage and parents approve genital surgery. In addition, some intersex activists believe a dismantling of the sex and gender binary will help them gain greater acceptance. Finally, many intersex activists believe that traditional views about disability, in which differences are viewed as problems in need of a fix, create an additional impediment to changing current medical practices. Chapter 8 discusses these viewpoints and provides a history of the development of the strategies the intersex movement has employed.

Chapters 9 and 10 explore the potential for advancing the intersex movement's goals by adopting legal strategies developed by other social justice movements that focus on ending discrimination based on sex, gender, sexual orientation, gender identity, and disability. Chapter 9 describes the historical efforts of different social justice movements that focus on issues related to sex and gender to form alliances. It examines the problems that have arisen among the intersex movement, feminists, lesbians, gays, and transsexuals and the potential for developing alliances and joint legal strategies that could benefit all these groups. Chapter 10 builds on chapter 9 by discussing the legal arguments that other social justice movements have employed successfully and exploring whether the intersex movement could benefit from adopting similar approaches.

# 8

# The History and Development of the Intersex Movement

The intersex activist movement was born in the 1990s. In its relatively short history, the movement has undergone significant transformation. Developing strategies to help accomplish the intersex movement's goals requires an understanding of its history and development.

## *The Start of the Movement*

The intersex activist movement was born in 1993 when Bo Laurent (formerly known as Cheryl Chase)[1] formed the Intersex Society of North America (ISNA). At its inception, ISNA had two goals. It wanted to provide a support network for people with an intersex condition and to develop strategies to challenge the traditional medical protocol for the treatment of infants born with an intersex condition.

To develop a support network, ISNA published a newsletter entitled *Hermaphrodites with Attitude*, which proclaimed itself the "world's only newsletter by and for intersexuals." Similar to other social justice movements, ISNA sought to reclaim and recharacterize the pejorative term applied to intersex people. In its initial newsletter, ISNA explained its desire to take the shame and secrecy that "hermaphrodites" had experienced and turn the term into one of empowerment:

> The word hermaphrodite is one which has been, for many of us, associated with deep pain and stigma. Physicians whose careers are dedicated to erasing intersexuality . . . characterize the birth of an intersexual infant as a "social emergency," and a traumatic emotional shock for the parents. . . . I believe that it is time for us to counter physicians' assertion that life as a hermaphrodite would be worthless, by embracing the word and asserting our own identity as hermaphrodites.[2]

Thus, the intersex movement began in a similar fashion to other social justice movements of the twentieth century. It sought to remove the shame and stigma associated with group membership and to provide a support network for individuals with common experiences, grievances, and concerns. At ISNA's inception, its goal was not limited to providing peer support to its members; it also wanted to challenge the standard medical protocol governing the treatment of infants born with an intersex condition. Activists challenged medical practices that they believed were based on producing heterosexual children with "normal" sex conforming bodies at the expense of sexual pleasure. They argued that no proof existed that these early genital surgeries saved children from psychological trauma and that in fact the procedures often led to shame and psychic harm as well as physical problems.

As a newly formed movement, ISNA sought the assistance of other organizations that it believed would share common concerns and goals. ISNA associated with gay and AIDS activist groups and adopted some of their tactics, including protests at medical gatherings. The group also worked closely with the Gay and Lesbian Alliance against Defamation (GLAD), the International Gay and Lesbian Human Rights Commission (IGLHRC), and the Gay and Lesbian Medical Association (GLMA).[3]

In one of ISNA's early newsletters, Eli Nevada and Cheryl Chase compared the struggles of the intersex community with the problems facing transsexuals:

> The emergence of a vocal intersex community follows a natural progression in the evolution of civil rights struggles. Race was followed by sex (feminism), then sexual orientation, and identity (transgender movement). The newly emerging intersexual minority carries the battle to the ground of embodiment.
>
> Anthropologist Gayle Rubin has written, "Sexualities keep marching out of the Diagnostic and Statistical Manual and onto the pages of social history . . . trying to emulate the successes of homosexuals." As we embark on our plan to march out of the Endocrinology textbooks, we must tip our hats to the transgender community for preparing the way for us. . . .
>
> We share [with the transgender community] the issue of self-determination: the right of the individual to choose. . . .
>
> Most of us, intersexual or transsexual, feels rage over how we have been treated. At times it is hard to know where to focus this anger. Our common enemy is the society that denies the individual the right to decide for themselves who they are and how they want to live their life. . . .

Those of us whose bodies cannot be easily categorized into the either/ or binary system automatically transgress this code of silence.

The heterosexist, dualistic system is built on a shaky foundation of lies and half truths . . . It is based upon a lie: that in the natural world, each person is born either male or female.[4]

Accomplishments by women's health movements and patient health movements also helped the intersex movement develop a framework for accomplishing its medical goals. These movements promoted patient autonomy and challenged the power of physicians to control decision making.[5]

ISNA also tried to work with feminists in the United States who were seeking legislation banning female genital cutting. As discussed in more detail in the next chapter, these efforts were not productive. Feminists seeking legislation banning female genital cutting as it is practiced by some Asian and African immigrants did not respond to ISNA's requests to expand the ban to include genital surgeries on infants with an intersex condition performed by Western doctors.[6] The exclusion of surgeries performed on infants with an intersex condition can be seen in the Federal Prohibition of Female Genital Mutilation Act of 1995, which specifically excludes from the ban on genital cutting procedures "necessary to the person's health . . . performed by a person licensed (in the place of its performance) as a medical practitioner."[7] In other words, the law continues to allow doctors to surgically alter an infant's genitalia if the doctor believes it is necessary to the child's psychological health.

Although ISNA was successful in forming a support network, during its early years it experienced limited success in convincing doctors to change their medical practices or even to listen to the concerns that intersex activists were expressing.

## The Growth of the Movement

By the late 1990s, due to a number of events, the intersex movement's influence had grown exponentially. Scholars outside of medicine began to write about intersexuality and the discourse broadened to include a number of arguments against the dominant treatment protocol. In addition, the Constitutional Court of Colombia issued the first decision from a country's highest court declaring that the dominant treatment protocol violated the human rights of infants born with an intersex condition. Finally, the report about David Reimer's treatment captured media attention and led to a number of television programs about the subject.[8]

Scholarly publications on intersexuality outside of the medical arena blossomed during this time. Suzanne Kessler, a social psychologist, began to question the underlying sex and gender assumptions of the intersex treatment protocol. She wrote an article in 1990 that called into question the naturalness of our binary gender system.[9] She also challenged the heteronormative beliefs justifying the standard medical protocol that emphasized the ability to engage in heterosexual intercourse. She expanded her critique in 1998 when she published *Lessons from the Intersexed*.[10] Anne Fausto-Sterling, a feminist scholar and biologist, also published an article calling into question society's binary sex classification system that ignores the existence of people with an intersex condition.[11] She further developed her critique of the intersex treatment protocol and the meanings of masculinity, femininity, homosexuality, and heterosexuality in her book *Sexing the Body: Gender Politics and the Construction of Sexuality*.[12] In 1998, Alice Domurat Dreger published *Hermaphrodites and the Medical Invention of Sex*, which challenged the medical treatment protocol by placing it into its historical context.[13] Although these and other publications from diverse disciplines provided persuasive arguments for reexamining the traditional treatment model, they did not appear to alter medical practices significantly.

During the late 1990s, legal scholars began to publish articles on the topic and the activist movement began incorporating legal arguments into their publications.[14] These publications broadened the framework to include allegations that medical practices violated basic civil rights, human rights, and children's rights. It was these types of legal arguments that were advanced in ISNA's briefs to the Colombia Constitutional Court that led the court to rule that the traditional medical protocol violated the fundamental human rights of infants with an intersex condition.[15]

One event, the exposure of the true story of David Reimer in academic literature and then in the popular press, provided the hook to lure media attention to intersexuality. As discussed in more detail in chapter 1, David Reimer, a male, lost his penis when he was eight months old during a botched circumcision. Based on medical advice, his parents decided to raise David as a girl. The parents allowed doctors to surgically alter his genitalia to conform to a female norm and to administer female hormones so that David (who was then called Brenda) would develop a female phenotype. For years, David's story was reported as a successful sex transformation. In 1997, Drs. Milton Diamond and Keith Sigmundson found David and exposed the fact that he had never identified as a girl and that he was living as a male.[16] Their report, and the later publication of the book *As Nature Made Him*, by John Colapinto,[17] caused society and medical practitioners to question the theory that gender identity is malleable. National media outlets, including *Newsweek*, the *New York Times*, *Rolling Stone*, *Mademoiselle*, NPR, *Dateline NBC*, and *Primetime ABC*, all presented stories sympathetic to the intersex movement's goals.[18]

## The Current Movement: Alternate Strategies for Accomplishing Common Goals

Intersex activism, scientific publications, and media coverage have led to one significant change in medical practices: most doctors no longer believe that infants are born without an innate sense of gender identity. Therefore, default female gender assignment is no longer the norm. Instead, in most cases, experts determine the likely gender identity of an infant with an intersex condition based on the etiology of the intersex condition and other factors and they recommend that the child be raised in that gender role. A consensus is emerging that an infant is likely to develop a male gender identity if he has a Y chromosome and testes and is sensitive to the influence of androgens. Most doctors are now suggesting that these children be raised as males.[19]

Other medical practices opposed by intersex activists continue. Intersex activists are still working (1) to end or limit cosmetic genital surgeries for infants born with an anatomy that someone has decided does not meet a male or female norm, (2) to stop the shame and secrecy surrounding the birth of a child with an intersex condition, and (3) to develop appropriate support and counseling systems for people with an intersex condition and their family members.

Intersex activists do not share a unified vision regarding the most effective strategies for accomplishing these goals. Developing effective frameworks for protecting individuals with an intersex condition has become a growing topic of discussion within the intersex movement. The debates have focused on a number of issues, including

- whether forming closer alliances with the medical community is desirable;
- whether utilizing a disability framework will effectively advance the rights of people with an intersex condition; and
- whether the movement should adopt or distance itself from an identity politics model.

## Forming Alliances with the Medical Community

Recently, some intersex activists have concluded that the initial strategies they used to challenge medical practices, including picketing medical conventions, are no longer necessary and are, in fact, counterproductive. They believe that forming alliances with physicians is the most effective means for influencing and changing medical practices. The 2006 Consensus Statement is an example of a productive alliance between physicians and activists. By working together, activists and medical experts formulated an approach that reflected a number of goals of the intersex activist movement, as noted on the ISNA website:

Although it is far from perfect, some of the ground-breaking changes advocated in the Consensus Statement (CS) include:

- *Progress in patient-centered care*: The CS states that psychosocial support is integral to care, that ongoing open communication with patients and families is essential and that it helps with well-being; that genital exams and medical photography should be limited; and that care should be more focused on addressing stigma not solely gender assignment and genital appearance.
- *More cautious approach to surgery*: The CS recommends no vaginoplasty in children; clitoroplasty only in more "severe" cases; and no vaginal dilation before puberty. It also states that the functional outcome of genital surgeries should be emphasized, not just cosmetic appearance. Perhaps most important it acknowledges there is no evidence that early surgery relieves parental distress.
- *Getting rid of misleading language*: By getting rid of a nomenclature based on "hermaphroditism," our hope is that this shift will help clinicians move away from the almost exclusive focus on gender and genitals to the real medical problems people with DSD [disorders of sex development] face. Improving care can now be framed as healthcare quality improvement, something medical professionals understand and find compelling.[20]

The problem is that no institution has fully adopted these proposals. In addition, as institutions maintain or modify their treatment protocol, no mechanism exists to assess the effectiveness of the different approaches. This concern led ISNA to close its doors in 2008 and to assist in the formation of a new organization, Accord Alliance, which would be responsible for accomplishing these goals. In ISNA's parting letter, it explained its reasons for changing its strategy:

> This is ISNA's dilemma: we finally have consensus on improvements to care for which we have advocated for so long, but we lack a consistent way to implement, monitor, and evaluate them. At present, the new standard of care exists as little more than ideals on paper, thus falling short of its aim to improve the lives of people with DSDs and their families.
>
> In the current environment, there is a strong need for an organization to assume the role of a convener of stakeholders across the health care system and DSD communities. It's the primary gap between today's status quo and the wide-spread implementation of the new standard of care we envision.
>
> Unfortunately, ISNA is considerably hamstrung in being able to fulfill this role. Although it has been very successful in recent years in creating collaborative relationships (our participation in the Intersex Consensus Group and authorship of the influential DSD Guideline handbooks being our most salient examples), there is concern among many healthcare professionals, parents, and mainstream healthcare system funders that ISNA's views are biased or that an association with ISNA will be frowned upon by colleagues and peers. And there is widespread misinformation about ISNA's positions.
>
> For ISNA and many of our collaborators, this has been extraordinarily frustrating and has hindered our ability to champion and move forward in this important work.
>
> We believe the most fruitful way to move beyond the current dynamic is to support a new organization with a mission to promote integrated, comprehensive approaches to care that enhance the overall health and well-being of persons with DSDs and their families.[21]

Accord Alliance began operations in March 2008 with the goal of "partnering with patients and families, healthcare administrators, providers, and researchers to facilitate open communication and collaboration among all persons working together to improve care."[22]

Other intersex activists do not support the strategy of working more closely with physicians. Some activists reject the idea of working side by side with the doctors who have made the decisions that have led to the current practices. They challenge the medicalization of intersex conditions and believe that collaboration with the medical community is counter to what they see as the more important goal of depathologizing gender nonconformity.[23]

Finally, some activists and organizations believe that a middle-ground approach may be more effective. They believe that they need to continue to challenge the medical community to improve its practices and procedures, but they also support creating a more productive dialogue with medical researchers and practitioners.[24]

### Using a Disability Framework: Changing Terminology from Intersex to DSD

Closely related to the debate about whether to form alliances with the medical community is the dispute about appropriate terminology. The 2006 Consensus Statement and some intersex organizations recommend that the term *intersex* be abandoned in favor of the term *disorders of sex development* (*DSD*). The suggested transition to the use of the term *DSD* has not met with universal support.

Those who support abandoning the term *intersex* do so for a number of reasons. Some believe that the label itself reinforces the current medical protocol that emphasizes the need for surgical and hormonal fixes. Bioethicists Ellen Feder and Katrina Karkazis have pointed out that the term *intersexuality* does not accurately describe a medical condition. Instead, the term *intersex* tends to create images of people who are abnormal because they are both male and female or neither male nor female. Intersexuality (being between the sexes) thus became the problem to be fixed. Rather than treating any physical or psychological complications inherent in the underlying condition, the goal became erasing the condition itself by surgical intervention. Those who advocate in favor of abandoning the term *intersexuality* believe that it may shift medical attention away from creating a "normal" appearance and move the focus to patients' well-being, which should be the goal of all medical practices.[25]

Supporters of the move to the DSD terminology have also argued that the term *intersex* is ambiguous and has led to arguments about who should be considered part of the movement. Some people with medical conditions not traditionally classified as intersex sought inclusion in the movement because they had suffered similar harms of traumatic surgeries, shame, and hiding.[26] On the other hand, some people, especially parents, did not like the label *intersex* and resented having their child labeled *intersex*. These people tried to limit the group included in the intersex classification. Some parents argued that the intersex classification should only apply to people with ambiguous genitalia or those with an unclear gender identity. Others asserted that *intersex* should refer only to conditions in which the chromosomes and phenotype are discordant. Some parents whose children had undergone surgery believed that their children may have been born with an intersex condition, but after surgery they were no longer intersex.[27]

Many parents dislike the term *intersex* because they believe it implies that their child is "in between" sexes or is transsexual. In addition, many parents do not want an "identity" forced on their child, especially if it is a "queer" identity to which the parents do not relate. Finally, the term *intersex* has the potential to sexualize their children, making it an issue of eroticism rather than biology.

Activists who support abandoning the term *intersex* are concerned that use of the term results in more surgeries being performed as parents seek to turn their "intersex" child into a "normal" heterosexual boy or girl.[28] In addition, use of a term that many people find objectionable makes building a broader cohesive movement more difficult.

In contrast, some activists reject the change in terminology. They believe that other than the few intersex conditions that pose an actual health risk, intersexuality is a not a medical condition. They reject further medicalization by using the term *DSD* because they believe that the label *disorder* may lead to more surgeries. They also believe that the term *disorder* is inappropriate because it is pejorative and they do not want to be labeled *disordered*. Finally, they prefer the term *intersexuality* because they want to continue to promote an intersex identity and culture.

Some people who support the move away from the term *intersex* but who also oppose the use of the term *disorder* have suggested alternate terminology, including *differences of sex development*[29] and *divergence of sex development*.[30]

The key unanswered question, however, is whether use of the term *disorder* will diminish the number of surgeries being performed. Although those who support the change in terminology believe that it will accomplish this goal, those who oppose the term are concerned that the label *disorder* will have the opposite effect and will lead to a perceived need to bring order to a disordered body. It is far too early to know which terminology will be the most effective tool for decreasing the number of medically unnecessary surgeries and ending the shame and secrecy surrounding the birth of a child with an intersex condition.

## Intersex as an Identity Movement

The intersex movement began as an identity movement and sought alliances with other identity movements with common concerns, including feminists and LGBT organizations. Currently, disagreements within the movement have arisen about whether to continue on the identity path and, if so, whether to align with other identity movements.

Some activists who want to continue developing as an identity movement want to do so because they self-identify as intersex (as opposed to male or female) and would like *intersex* to be recognized as a third sex category.

*Chris was born with ovarian and testicular tissue. At puberty, Chris developed female breasts. Although Chris was raised as a male, he has physical attributes of both genders. More importantly, Chris identifies himself as neither male nor female and prefers to be called intersex. Chris's intersex identity is so important to him that he wanted to be legally married as an intersex person. Australia law recognizes only marriages between a man and a woman so Chris was not allowed to legally marry in his self-identified sex. Chris stated: "I would like the law and my marriage certificate to acknowledge my reality as an intersexed person."*[31]

Other intersex activists who support an identity movement model do not support the acceptance of a "third sex." Nonetheless, they do speak about intersexuality as a form of identity. For example, Organisation Intersex International (OII) talks about "intersex lives and experience by highlighting the richness of intersex identities and cultures."[32] OII does not advocate that the law recognize a third sex, but it does seek to help "people to understand that there are not just two pre-existing sexes. There is an infinite combination of possibilities on the spectrum of sex and gender."[33] OII and similar organizations believe that the most effective means to protect people with an intersex condition from harm is to improve societal acceptance of sex and gender variations.

In contrast to OII and others who associate strongly with their intersex identity, some activists believe that intersexuality is a condition (or disorder) and does not reflect a person's "identity." Many individuals who accept that they have a DSD do not identify as intersex and are offended when the term is applied to them. They have rejected identity politics as an effective means for advancing the movement's goals.[34]

On the other hand, a number of intersex activists who support an identity politics approach feel closely aligned with the LGBT community. LGBT activism, by challenging legal and societal notions of appropriate sex and gender behavior, laid the foundation for the first challenges to the medical protocol for infants with an intersex condition. Surgeries on infants with atypical genitalia have been justified based on a narrow view of acceptable sex anatomies and gender behavior. Successful LGBT challenges to sex and gender norms thus helped to frame the arguments against early genital surgery.[35]

Unfortunately, it is these societal norms that have led some activists to want to distance themselves from gay and lesbian groups. Many adults with an intersex condition do not consider themselves gender "queer," especially if they identify as heterosexual. Therefore, they do not identify with gay and lesbian activist concerns. In addition, given that many parents want their children to be "normal heterosexuals," some intersex activists are concerned that linking the movement with gay organizations might prompt more parents to opt for surgical intervention.[36]

Being linked with the transsexual movement has proven to be even more controversial. As discussed at the beginning of this chapter, the intersex movement initially tipped its hat to the transsexual movement and focused on their commonalities. Now, some intersex advocates want to distance themselves from the transsexual movement for two reasons. First, they want to maintain the movement's focus on the trauma and stigma that early genital surgeries cause rather than on the issue of gender identity. In addition, some intersex activists believe that some transsexual organizations have co-opted the term *intersex* for their own benefit without carefully considering the negative effect their actions might have on people with an intersex condition.

The intersex movement, like other social justice movements, has struggled to develop the most beneficial advocacy frameworks and to create the most effective alliances to accomplish its objectives. The goal shared by all who are concerned about people with an intersex condition is to enhance their physical and emotional well-being and to end the shame and stigma that persons with an intersex condition endure.

Whether to associate with the medical community, the disability community, feminists, or LGBT organizations is a question that produces divergent viewpoints within the intersex community. To help understand the advantages and disadvantages of forming alliances with other social justice movements, chapter 9 chronicles the history of the conflicts that have arisen among other social justice movements that share similar concerns. Chapter 10 examines the various legal strategies that these movements have employed to advance their rights and to gain greater acceptance.

# 9

# Conflicts among Social Justice Movements with Common Concerns

As discussed in the previous chapter, intersex activists do not share identical visions about whether forming alliances with doctors, feminists, LGBT activists, or disability rights groups will be the most effective means to accomplish the movement's goals. Other social justice movements have been confronted with similar dilemmas. Examining some of the conflicts in the feminist and LGBT movements may shed light on the extent to which the intersex movement can achieve its goals through alliances with other social justice movements.

The first section of this chapter discusses the intersex movement's actions related to forming coalitions with feminist and LGBT organizations. Thus far, feminist groups have refused to address the issues that are central to the intersex community. On the other hand, LGBT organizations have welcomed an alliance with the intersex community. Some LGBT organizations have added an "I" to their acronym. This addition has too often been one in name only and has led to concerns in the intersex community.

The second section of this chapter focuses on conflicts that have arisen between feminist and lesbian activists, feminist and transsexual activists, and the LGB and transsexual communities. Some of these disagreements have been productively resolved, while others still continue to hamper progress. Understanding the nature of these conflicts may help the intersex movement avoid similar pitfalls as the movement develops.

## Relationships between the Intersex Movement and Other Social Justice Movements

### The Intersex and Feminist Movements

During the 1990s, the formative years of the intersex movement, people with an intersex condition found inspiration in feminist writings about the social construction of gender. Feminist theory provided a supportive framework for people whose gender identity did not conform to the sex assigned to them at birth, as well as for those who had developed an intersex identity. It also helped many people with an intersex condition understand how their medical treatment had been based on societal assumptions about appropriate genitalia and gender roles.[1]

Therefore, it came as quite a shock to the intersex community when a leading feminist, Germaine Greer, stated, "It is my considered position that femaleness is conferred by the final pair of XX chromosomes. Otherwise, I don't know what it is."[2] Some women with AIS (females with XY chromosomes) and family members of girls with AIS challenged her assumptions, but Greer refused to back down.[3]

The intersex movement also met rejection from feminists who worked to oppose female genital cutting (FGC) as it is practiced in non-Western countries. Western feminists fought against FGC for more than twenty-five years for a number of reasons. The practice results in pain, physical complications, and psychological harm. It typically impairs sexual pleasure and violates a girl's right to autonomy because it is often performed without proper consent. Most important, it is medically unnecessary and only serves to reinforce male cultural norms and patriarchal power.[4] Anti-FGC feminists have succeeded in getting the practice banned or condemned by the United Nations,[5] the U.S. Congress,[6] U.S. state legislatures,[7] and a number of other countries.[8]

The reasons for opposing genital surgery on infants with an intersex condition are similar to the arguments made by feminists who are opposed to FGC. Surgeries on infants with an intersex condition and FGC often result in almost identical physical harms, including a loss or diminishment of erotic response, genital pain and discomfort, infections, scarring, urinary incontinence, and genitalia that are not cosmetically acceptable. In addition, they are both medically unnecessary and are performed without the informed consent of the patient.

Most important, just as FGC is used to reinforce gender norms, one of the goals of intersex surgeries is to reinforce heterosexism and cultural norms of appropriate gender roles. The traditional protocol for the surgical treatment of infants with an intersex condition is based on stereotypes regarding appropriate male and female sexual activity and reproductive capacity. A major priority for children raised as males is to ensure that they will be capable of engaging in heterosexual intercourse when they reach adulthood. Thus, doctors have turned XY infants into girls if they have believed that the XY child's phallus was inadequate for penetration. This surgery was performed even if it destroyed the child's ability to reproduce. In other words, for males, penetration of a vagina was prioritized above the ability to procreate.[9]

XX infants have been treated differently. Typically, an XX infant with a phallus larger than a typical clitoris, who is capable of bearing children, has had her reproductive capacity maintained. At the same time, her clitoris has been surgically reduced, even if such reduction could lead to a loss or impairment of sexual pleasure. In addition, an XX infant born with a vagina incapable of accommodating a penis typically undergoes surgery to construct a vaginal canal so that she will be capable of engaging in heterosexual intercourse. In other words, the traditional protocol for the treatment of infants with an intersex condition is based on the belief that it is more important for men to be able to engage in penetrative sex than to be able to reproduce and more important for women to be penetrated by a man and to be able to bear children, even if their ability to enjoy sex is impaired or destroyed.

Intersex activists believe that anti-FGC feminists and legislators adopting anti-FGC legislation should recognize the parallels between the harmful practices of FGC and genital surgery performed on infants with an intersex condition. When Congress was considering the Female Genital Mutilation Act, intersex activists and academics wrote to Congresswoman Patricia Schroeder, the principal author of the bill, asking that the language be modified to include a ban on surgeries being performed on infants with an intersex condition. They did not receive a reply from Congresswoman Schroeder.[10] Intersex activists also asked anti-FGC feminist groups to help them convince legislatures to include infant intersex genital surgeries within the ban on FGC.[11] Despite the similarities between the surgeries, their harmful physical and psychological effects, and the patriarchal heterosexist norms that support both practices, anti-FGC feminists have excluded intersex concerns from their agenda. Western feminist organizations that oppose FGC have refused to challenge Western doctors who perform surgery on infants with an intersex condition.[12]

Another medical practice affecting fetuses that may have an intersex condition illustrates why feminists should be concerned about how infants with an intersex condition are being treated. Some doctors are administering dexamethasone to pregnant women who may be carrying a child with congenital adrenal hyperplasia (CAH). The purpose of the treatment is to "feminize" girls with an intersex condition. Although the major stated purpose of this treatment is to stop the genitalia from masculinizing, researchers have also noted that a potential beneficial side effect of this dangerous medication may be to enhance feminine thinking and behavior. Women with CAH have a higher likelihood of being bisexual or lesbian and often display behavior that is considered "tomboyish." Some researchers have implied that administration of dexamethasone to pregnant women may solve this "problem." One study reports,

> CAH women as a group have a lower interest than controls in getting married and performing the traditional child-care/housewife role. As children, they show an unusually low interest in engaging in maternal play with baby dolls, and their interest in caring for infants, the frequency of daydreams or fantasies of pregnancy and motherhood, or the expressed wish of experiencing pregnancy and having children of their own appear to be relatively low in all age groups. . . . Long term follow-up studies of the behavioral outcome will show whether dexamethasone treatment also prevents the effects of prenatal androgens on brain and behavior.[13]

In other words, some doctors are suggesting that they could be assisting girls by administering a drug to their pregnant mothers that will turn the fetus into a woman who will want to fulfill the traditional female roles of housewife and mother.

Feminists have mounted challenges to practices they believe hinder the ability of women to participate fully in society. They have focused their efforts on ending discrimination based on sex stereotypes and respecting a woman's right to bodily autonomy. Treatment protocols for intersexuality are partially based on stereotypes about the proper role for women. In addition, they involve invasive and irreversible procedures implicating the right to bodily autonomy. Despite the fact that some intersex treatment protocols are based on sex stereotypes that have been the target of the feminist movement for decades, feminist organizations have failed to include the issues of the intersex community on their agenda and direct overtures by the intersex community to feminist leaders have been ignored.

The Intersex and LGBT Movements

The LGBT movement, and especially transsexuals, laid much of the groundwork for the intersex movement. Early intersex activists began their work by building on strategies employed by the LGBT community. LGBT groups have supported the intersex movement in a number of ways. They have provided the bulk of the limited funding for intersex-specific organizations. In addition, LGBT leaders have provided critical training and support to intersex community leaders.

The intersex and LGBT communities share a number of concerns. Both suffer from public misperceptions and misinformation, experience shame, engage in secrecy and hiding, and endure oppression as a result of the gender binary system. In addition, people with an intersex condition and transsexuals may be confronted by similar problems in housing, participation in athletic competitions, locker room use, and access to public bathrooms.

The medical community's treatment of transsexual adults and infants with an intersex condition is also based on similar assumptions. The standard treatment protocol for infants with an intersex condition is based on the desire to reinforce heterosexism and cultural norms of appropriate gender roles. Similar stereotypes have been applied to transsexual adults seeking medical assistance. Transsexuals have often had to convince doctors that they conform to rigid heterosexual and gender norms before physicians will agree to provide treatment.[14] People with an intersex condition and transsexuals are sometimes forced to cede control over their bodies to medical "experts."

The transsexual and intersex movements' concerns also overlap because a number of people with an intersex condition choose to live in the sex opposite to the one assigned to them at birth. According to one study, 24 percent of the people with an intersex condition interviewed developed a gender identity that did not conform to the sex assigned to them at birth.[15]

Despite the close connections between the intersex and LGBT communities, a number of intersex activists now want to distance the intersex movement from LGBT organizations and oppose adding "I" to the LGBT acronym for a number of reasons.[16]

Some intersex activists fear that adding "I" would convey the false impression that all or most intersex people are lesbian, gay, bisexual, or transsexual. They believe that such an inappropriate conflation may lead parents to choose surgery to ease their own concerns about their child's future gender identity or sexual orientation.[17]

In addition, some intersex activists are concerned that the issues central to the intersex movement are not reflected in the agendas of many LGBT organizations. The major LGBT groups tend to focus a significant portion of their resources on legalizing same-sex marriage, punishing hate crimes, and protecting gays and lesbians from employment discrimination. Some intersex activists are concerned that the real battles facing the intersex community are too far removed from these causes.[18]

Furthermore, as LGBT organizations advocate in favor of same-sex marriage, they sometimes use the existence of intersexuality to bolster their claims. Some intersex activists fear that the resulting backlash to the same-sex marriage movement may inadvertently harm the intersex community. For example, in California, in response to the strong movement in favor of same-sex marriage, anti-same-sex-marriage advocates proposed a voter initiative that would limit marriage to one man and one woman. The proposed initiative defined a man as a person with a Y chromosome.[19] Although this law was not adopted, some intersex activists are concerned that additional backlash to the same-sex marriage movement may threaten the marriages of some men and women with an intersex condition whose chromosomal structures do not match the typical pattern.

Some intersex activists are also concerned about whether the limited resources available to LGBT organizations will be used to advance the issues that are most important to the intersex community. They believe that if LGBT organizations add the "I" without truly incorporating intersex issues on their agenda, donors may mistakenly believe that they are supporting the intersex movement. Funds that may otherwise be donated to organizations focusing on issues central to the intersex community may thus be diverted.

Finally, LGBT activism has developed as part of an identity movement, with shared community concerns. Some people in the intersex movement identify as intersex and want to develop a similar intersex community and form alliances with LGBT groups, but many intersex activists view intersexuality as a medical condition and not as an issue of identity.

Emi Koyama, a well-respected and prominent intersex activist, has advised LGBT organizations about adding an "I" to their name:

> [W]hat can be said about whether or not to add the "I"? I feel that we should take a pragmatic approach. If adding the "I" would enable you to put your energy and resources onto doing more things that help the intersex movement, then by all means add the "I." If adding the "I" will help you become a better resource for people with intersex conditions, then

do it. You might make some intersex people angry, but at least you are doing something concrete to help end shame, secrecy and isolation that are imposed on intersex children.

But do not think that adding the "I" as an empty gesture is by itself an achievement. Adding "intersex" to an LGBT group must mean a commitment to take concrete actions to address the specific needs of intersex people; anything less is tokenism, or a mere fashion statement, which will not benefit the intersex movement.[20]

## Conflicts among Other Sex, Gender, and Sexual Orientation Movements

The tensions that have arisen between the intersex community and the feminist and LGBT movements mirror similar conflicts that have plagued most social justice movements. For example, in the early years of the feminist movement, second-wave feminists purposefully excluded lesbian issues from the feminist agenda and some feminists referred to lesbians as "the lavender menace." These feminists were concerned that inclusion of lesbians would hamper the movement's ability to achieve the gender equality that they sought. In 1970, at the gathering of the Second Congress to Unite Women, a group of lesbians was enraged at the exclusion of lesbian concerns. Their protest led to a discussion of the experience of lesbianism in a heterosexist culture and the adoption of four prolesbian resolutions. As the feminist movement matured, lesbians became more fully incorporated in the membership of feminist organizations and issues directly affecting lesbians became part of the feminist agenda.[21]

Many feminists were even more opposed to the inclusion of transsexuals than they were to incorporating lesbians into the women's movement. This aversion to including transsexuals in some female spaces still exists. Some feminists have raised three justifications for excluding transsexuals and their concerns from the feminist movement. They argue that male-to-female transsexuals should be excluded from feminist groups because they continue to have access to the power associated with their male-privileged upbringing and cannot truly identify with the subordinated position of women who have been raised as females. Some feminists assert that female-to-male transsexuals should be excluded from feminist spaces because they have rejected their womanhood to gain the advantages awarded to men in society's patriarchal system. Finally, and probably most important, some feminists believe that transsexuals have bought into essentialist notions of sex and gender and inappropriately seek to cross the gender divide rather than to deconstruct it.[22]

Feminist demonization of transsexuals reached its height during the 1970s and 1980s when Janice Raymond and Mary Daly, two prominent lesbian feminists, argued that transsexualism is equivalent to necrophilia and rape. Raymond and Daly played a significant role in closing many clinics that serviced transsexuals and their writings influenced many others in the feminist movement.[23]

A number of feminist gatherings chose to exclude transsexuals. For example, the Michigan Womyn's Music Festival (MWMF), one of the largest annual social gatherings of women, forcefully ejected a male-to-female transsexual attendee in 1991 when she identified herself in a workshop as a transsexual woman. In 1992, the festival added to its website its "womyn-born-womyn" policy. The 1991 Lesbian Conference in Atlanta also discriminated against transsexuals by only allowing genetic women to attend.[24]

Younger women, many of whom were born during the 1960s and 1970s and who self-identify as third-wave feminists, are not as critical of transsexuals as were second-wave feminists. Some find it difficult, however, to identify with transsexual claims. Daughters of second-wave feminists were typically taught that gender would not play a role in determining their future success. Therefore, some younger women find it difficult to relate to people who would want to transition to the opposite sex. They question how people could assign gender such critical importance that it would become the defining feature of their identity.[25]

Many feminist activists have moved away from their original outright rejection of and animosity toward transsexuals. But many feminists still fail to understand transsexual concerns and transsexuals are far from fully incorporated into the feminist movement.

Similar problems have occurred surrounding the inclusion of transsexuals in the lesbian, gay, and bisexual movement. Most transsexuals believe that the gay/lesbian/bisexual and transsexual movements are inseparable. A significant number of transsexuals also identify as lesbian, gay, or bisexual. More important, they recognize that homophobia and transphobia are closely linked and that bias and violence against both groups is motivated by animosity toward those who transgress gender norms.[26]

Although transsexuals were on the front lines at Stonewall in 1969 and played a pivotal role in launching the modern gay rights movement, some gay and lesbian organizations have not fully incorporated transsexuals into the LGB movement. As the gay and lesbian movement developed, transsexuals and their issues often were marginalized or completely ignored. During the 1970s and 1980s, transsexual concerns rarely appeared in LGB organizations' mission statements. Many gays and lesbians viewed transsexuals' claims as valid but unrelated to the gay and lesbian movement. They did not understand the connection between gay and transsexual rights and believed that trying to combine these two diverse issues would lead to a loss of focus and effectiveness.[27]

Some LGB activists believe that incorporating transsexual concerns into the modern gay movement could compromise the movement's main strategy of seeking incremental progress. These activists argue that aside from their sexual orientation, gays and lesbians are just like heterosexuals in every other way, including their gender presentation. Therefore, they have adopted a strategy of asserting that their minor difference (their sexual orientation) cannot be used to deny them the same legal rights and protections provided to heterosexuals. Because the modern gay movement has been built on projecting an image of conformity, some lesbian and gay activists believe that including transsexual issues could threaten their overall strategy.[28]

This issue came to a head in 2007 when the United States Congress considered a bill that would have prohibited discrimination based on sexual orientation. The original version of the bill also prohibited discrimination based on gender identity and expression. When it appeared that a transgender inclusive Employment Nondiscrimination Act (ENDA) would not pass, Congressman Barney Frank proposed a bill that deleted the "gender identity and expression" language.

In a watershed moment for the LGBT movement, all the major LGBT organizations, except the Human Rights Campaign (HRC), joined forces to oppose the new version. They united together to oppose the passage of any bill that failed to protect transsexuals along with gays and lesbians. Gay and lesbian activists stood side by side with their transsexual siblings and refused to accept legal rights that they had spent decades fighting for unless the laws prohibited discrimination based on gender identity and expression as well as sexual orientation. Congress has not yet passed any version of ENDA.[29]

Conflicts among feminists, lesbian, gay, transsexual, and intersex groups are similar to disagreements that have arisen among other civil rights organizations. Progressive social movements based on identity politics have suffered from external systems of subordination. Rights are often framed as limited commodities. Those who oppose expanding rights to marginalized groups often pit one group against another, using a divide-and-conquer strategy based on perceived conflicts of interest. Progress is also inhibited by the reality that genuine and substantial conflicts within and between groups exist.

Each time an organization's umbrella is expanded to include other marginalized groups, it may become more difficult to effectively accomplish the organization's broadened goals with the limited resources available. Internal and external divisions can potentially hamper a social justice movement's forward progress.

The harms suffered by people with an intersex condition, women, gays, lesbians, and transsexuals are not identical and cannot be easily subsumed under one umbrella. Homophobia, transphobia, and sexism, however, are intertwined as part of an overall cultural system of patriarchy, heterosexism, and rigid binary sex and gender norms that inhibit the full equality of women, LGBTs, and people with an intersex condition.

The next chapter analyzes three potential legal frameworks effectively employed by other progressive social justice movements—human rights, disability rights, and sex discrimination—that may help the intersex movement accomplish its goals. The concluding chapter explores the potential for forming effective alliances to help the intersex movement advance its agenda through the assertion of legal claims.

# 10

# Legal Frameworks

Lawsuits brought by or against people with an intersex condition have been rare. Two cases in Colombia challenged the ability of parents to consent to the performance of genital surgery on infants with an intersex condition;[1] one court in Australia determined whether an adolescent with an intersex condition should be allowed to transition from male to female;[2] one case in Germany allowed a woman to sue a doctor who had removed her internal reproductive organs without her consent;[3] two cases (one in England and one in Australia) involved the validity of a marriage in which one of the spouses had an intersex condition;[4] one employee with an intersex condition sued her employer for wrongful termination in the United States;[5] and two cases in the United States involved people with an intersex condition challenging the treatment they received when they were incarcerated.[6]

## *Lawsuits Involving People with an Intersex Condition Are Likely to Increase*

In the future, lawsuits involving people with an intersex condition are likely to increase for three reasons:

- Medical practices may be challenged in the United States and other countries as they were challenged in Colombia.
- As surgeries on infants with an intersex condition diminish, people with an intersex condition may be subjected to discriminatory practices that are currently directed against transsexuals.
- As governmental agencies adopt policies that are appropriate for transsexuals, they may inappropriately apply these rules to persons with an intersex condition.

## Challenges to Medical Practices

The current medical protocol supporting early genital cosmetic surgery is coming under increasing attack. At some point, court challenges are likely. Litigation could be initiated on behalf of a child who is about to undergo surgical intervention, by an adult who had been subjected to these procedures, or by parents or physicians seeking court approval because they are concerned about potential liability if they proceed without a court order.[7] Lawsuits brought by people with an intersex condition against doctors could take three forms. Doctors who perform surgery on a person with an intersex condition could be sued if they fail to fully inform the patient or the patient's parents and obtain proper informed consent, if they perform surgeries on infants that result in sterilization or that are invasive and irreversible without first seeking court review and approval, or if they fail to comply with acceptable medical practices.

## Challenges to Discriminatory Actions

As the number of infant genital surgeries declines, more people with an intersex condition may be subjected to discriminatory practices that are currently directed against transsexuals. Individuals whose genitalia do not conform to a clear male/female binary norm may have their legal sex challenged. Therefore, issues involving their right to marry in their self-identified gender role, to amend their identity documents, to have access to housing and facilities that match their gender identity, and to be free from discrimination based on their intersex status are more likely to develop.

## Challenges to Government Policies

Because most lawmakers do not understand the differences between intersexuality and transsexuality, they may develop rules for people with an intersex condition that are consistent with their policies affecting transsexuals. Often, these regulations may not be appropriate and someone with an intersex condition will inevitably challenge them. Anecdotal evidence indicates that these problems are already arising with identity documents (including birth certificates and passports) and insurance coverage.[8]

Anne Tamar-Mattis, director of Advocates for Informed Choice, the first organization to undertake a coordinated strategy of legal advocacy for the rights of children with intersex conditions, states,

We are seeing more cases where intersex people trying to change their identity documents are being caught in a net that was developed to stop transsexuals from amending their documents. In the past, many intersex people who needed to change identity documents were able to do so under the "clerical error" provisions of state regulations governing birth certificates. Typically, a doctor's letter stating that a mistake was made would be required, but many clerks would accept these physician statements at face value and amend the sex indicator on the birth certificate. Now that many states have adopted written procedures for addressing transsexuals' birth certificate amendment requests, bureaucrats automatically turn to those rules no matter how inappropriate or inapplicable they may be.[9]

The State Department's recently amended policy illustrates this problem. The State Department intended to make it easier for transsexuals to amend the sex marker on their passports. New rules went into effect in 2010 that allow transsexuals to obtain an amended passport by presenting a certificate from a medical physician stating that the applicant has undergone appropriate clinical treatment for gender transition. The new standards state that sex reassignment surgery is not a prerequisite for changing the gender marker and that such documentation should not be requested by government officials.[10]

For the first time, the State Department also addressed the ability of people with an intersex condition to amend their gender marker on their passport. The original version of the new rules indicated that the drafters did not fully understand intersexuality. They used inappropriate terminology such as "internal genitalia." Their definition of intersexuality did not include all intersex conditions. Finally, they required that people with an intersex condition undergo gender transition, based on a similar requirement for transsexuals, even though gender transition for people with an intersex condition would be inappropriate in many circumstances. It was only after intersex advocates critiqued the new rules that appropriate changes were made.[11]

In addition to people whose gender identity does not match the sex assigned on the birth record, as the intersex movement grows, some people with an intersex condition may choose not to be pigeon-holed into the male/female binary. Tamar-Mattis notes that she is seeing more people rejecting the labels *male* or *female*. Some people with an intersex condition would like to be legally recognized as intersex. Others may prefer not to have the state create a "legal" sex for them.[12]

These recent developments indicate that legal challenges involving people with an intersex condition are likely to increase dramatically.

## Theoretical Approaches Supporting Legal Reform

Convincing legal institutions to enhance the safeguards provided to infants with an intersex condition being subjected to cosmetic genital surgeries or to protect people with an intersex condition from discriminatory practices requires the development of persuasive legal frameworks. If a proposed surgical intervention on an infant or minor causes sterilization, courts should apply the same standards that they do to the sterilization of developmentally disabled people to ensure that the fundamental right to reproduction is protected.[13] To the extent that fundamental rights are not at stake, the intersex movement will need to develop persuasive legal frameworks to challenge medical practices and discriminatory actions. This chapter discusses three successful discrimination models employed by other progressive social justice movements that could provide the basis for a legal claim brought on behalf of a person with an intersex condition: human rights, disability rights, and discrimination based on sex, gender, or sexual orientation.

### Human Rights

#### The Human Rights Commission of the City of San Francisco
Only one human rights organization has considered whether the current treatment protocol for infants with an intersex condition violates these children's human rights. In 2005, the Human Rights Commission of the City of San Francisco published a comprehensive report critiquing the medical treatment of infants born with an intersex condition. After providing an extensive analysis of current medical practices, the commission concluded that medically unnecessary cosmetic genital surgeries, which the commission called "normalizing interventions," should not be performed. Its significant findings include the following:

2. "Normalizing" interventions done without the patient's informed consent are inherent human rights abuses.
3. "Normalizing" interventions deprive intersex people of the opportunity to express their own identity and to experience their own intact physiology.
4. It is unethical to disregard a child's intrinsic human rights to privacy, dignity, autonomy, and physical integrity by altering genitals through irreversible surgeries for purely psychosocial and aesthetic rationales. It is wrong to deprive a person of the right to determine their sexual experience and identity. . . .

10. "Normalizing" interventions performed to alleviate a parent's social discomfort about their child's intersex anatomy violate the patient's human rights.

11. "Normalizing" medical interventions performed on an intersex child to address the discomfort of doctors, relatives, and anyone other than the consenting patient is a violation of the child's human rights.[14]

The commission recommended that "normalizing" interventions be banned during infancy or childhood. Any procedures that are not medically necessary should occur only if patients, and not their parents, give their legal consent. Thus, the commission recommended that these procedures be delayed until children are able to determine for themselves whether they want to undergo any medical procedures.[15]

### The United Nations Convention on the Rights of the Child

Although no other human rights organization has specifically addressed whether the current treatment protocol for infants with an intersex condition violates any laws, treaties, or conventions, a number of United Nations Conventions contain general language protecting basic human rights.[16] The Convention on the Rights of the Child, which was adopted by the General Assembly of the United Nations on November 20, 1989, is the most applicable human rights convention for addressing the rights of children with an intersex condition.[17] The Convention could provide the legal basis in countries that have ratified it to challenge life altering surgeries that are performed without the informed consent of the person undergoing the surgery.

The Convention reaffirms children's special needs for legal safeguards and recognizes that children are vulnerable and require special care and protection. The Colombian Constitutional Court relied on the Convention in determining that the current medical protocol does not adequately protect a child's right to bodily autonomy. The dominant medical treatment protocol for infants with an intersex condition does not ensure the protection of an infant's fundamental human rights as defined in the Convention. Current medical practices regarding infants with an intersex condition may violate articles 2, 3, 12, and 16.

Article 2 prohibits discrimination against children on the basis of sex. Current medical practices may violate this requirement. Although practices have started to change, anecdotal evidence indicates that some doctors treat male and female infants differently. Some doctors still assume that it is more important for males to have a penis that will allow them to engage in penetrative sex with a female than for them to be able to procreate. Thus, an XY infant with a phallus that is deemed too small for penetrative sex in adulthood may be assigned the female sex. His genitalia would be altered to appear "female," and his testicles would be removed, even though such removal would sterilize an otherwise fertile male. For XX children, the need to procreate, rather than the ability to engage in satisfactory sexual intercourse, is still emphasized. An XX infant who is capable of reproducing typically is assigned the female sex to preserve her reproductive capability, regardless of the appearance of her external genitalia. If her "phallus" is considered too large to meet the guidelines for a typical clitoris, it is sometimes surgically reduced, even if the reduction reduces or destroys her capacity for satisfactory sex. In other words, males are being defined by their ability to penetrate and females are being defined by their ability to procreate. This protocol treats XY and XX children differently on the basis of gender stereotypes about the proper roles for men and women and could be considered a violation of article 2.

Article 3 requires that in all actions concerning children, the best interests of the child must be a primary consideration. The traditional medical protocol emphasizes the need to "normalize" the child. One of the motivations for "normalizing" the child is to ease the psychological discomfort of the parents and to enhance their ability to bond with their child. Surgical alteration of a child may result in involuntary sterilization, diminished capacity for sexual satisfaction, and a gender assignment that may be contrary to the child's gender identity. Therefore, the traditional protocol does not ensure that the best interests of the child are a primary consideration and thus may violate article 3.

Article 12 protects children's rights to have their opinion taken into account in any matter affecting them. The traditional protocol ensures that children do not have input into decisions that have a profound effect on their lives. They are being subjected to irreversible surgeries that may affect their ability to procreate and to achieve sexual satisfaction. These decisions are being made when the children are too young to participate in the decision making process and may violate their right to have their opinions considered on a life altering matter. Waiting until these children are old enough to meaningfully participate in the decision making process would ensure that article 12 is not violated.

Article 16 protects children from interference in their right to privacy. Procreative decisions are considered a fundamental privacy right under the United States Constitution[18] and the laws of many other nations. Surgeries that result in involuntary sterilization infringe on the child's fundamental right to privacy under article 16.

The Convention on the Rights of the Child provides enhanced safeguards to protect the rights of children. In nations that have ratified the Convention, legal institutions may determine that surgical alteration of children with an intersex condition, as practiced under the traditional model, improperly infringes on their basic human rights. Although the Convention has been almost universally ratified, it has not yet been ratified by the United States. (The only other nation that has failed to ratify the Convention is Somalia.) Therefore, although a children's rights framework could be used effectively in nations other than the United States, it may not provide the most persuasive basis for protecting children born with an intersex condition in the United States. Proceeding under a well defined antidiscrimination statute (based on either a disability or a sex/ gender discrimination framework) may prove to be a more successful avenue than adopting a human rights framework based on a children's rights model.

## Disability Rights

A disability model may prove to be a beneficial framework for protecting people with an intersex condition. Disability claims could be based on the United Nations Convention on the Rights of Persons with Disabilities, the Americans with Disabilities Act, and state statutes and regulations prohibiting disability discrimination.

### United Nations Convention on the Rights of Persons with Disabilities

The likelihood of success employing a disability rights model is enhanced now that the United States has agreed to become a signatory to the United Nations Convention on the Rights of Persons with Disabilities, a treaty that elevates disability beyond a health and social welfare issue to a human rights issue.[19] The treaty's goal is to "promote, protect and ensure the full and equal enjoyment of all human rights and fundamental freedoms by all persons with disabilities, and to promote respect for their inherent dignity." The treaty includes the right to equality under the law; the right to live in the community; the right to education, health, and work; the right to participate in political, public, and cultural life; and most important for children with an intersex condition, the right to health care without discrimination.[20]

*The Americans with Disabilities Act*

The Americans with Disabilities Act (ADA) provides the primary avenue in the United States for pursuing a disability claim.[21] This federal law prohibits discrimination against a person with a disability in a number of areas, including the provision of health services.[22]

Thus far, no one with an intersex condition has brought a claim under the ADA or other disability statutes. These statutes may provide an avenue for limiting surgical alterations of infants with an intersex condition and eliminating the stigma associated with such conditions. In addition, to the extent that people with an intersex condition suffer from other discriminatory actions, the ADA may protect them.

Section 12102(1) of the ADA provides the basic ADA rules. This section defines disability as follows:

(A)  A physical or mental impairment that substantially limits one or more major life activities of such individual;

(B)  A record of such an impairment; or

(C)  Being regarded as having such an impairment (as described in paragraph (3)).[23]

*Physical impairment*: Some intersex conditions create medical risks that qualify as an actual impairment under section 12102(1)(A). For example, people with an intersex condition that impairs the endocrine and bladder functions or results in infertility meet the definition of a physical impairment under this section.[24] Many people with an intersex condition are not impaired. They are able to live full productive lives without medical intervention. These individuals would be protected under section 12102(1)(C), however, if they are subjected to surgeries or discriminatory actions because they are "regarded as having such an impairment."

*Regarded as having such an impairment*: Doctors performing cosmetic genital surgery on infants with an intersex condition do so for a number of reasons. They assert that children who grow up with atypical genitalia will suffer emotional trauma. In addition, they believe that adults with atypical genitalia will face obstacles in forming romantic relationships or engaging in reproductive or other sexual acts. These children are not actually impaired and are able to participate in all major life activities without medical intervention. Despite the fact that they are not actually impaired, they are often subjected to life-alerting surgical interventions to conform their bodies to a binary sex norm on the basis of the unsupported assumption that atypical genitalia and reproductive systems will limit the ability to engage in satisfactory sexual relationships in adulthood.[25] The medical treatment protocol for infants with an intersex condition is based on the perception that they are impaired. This differential treatment could meet the requirements of section 12102(1)(C).

*Actual or perceived limitation of a major life activity:* Major life activities under the ADA include operations of major bodily functions, including but not limited to functions of the bladder, the endocrine system, and the reproductive system.[26] Therefore, people with an intersex condition that affects these functions meet the requirement of a limitation of a major life activity. People with an intersex condition that does not affect these functions are unlikely to be limited from participating in any major life activities. Therefore, they would not meet the requirements of section 12102(1)(A). They could still meet the act's requirements under section 12102(3), which provides that for purposes of section 12102(1)(C), "[a]n individual meets the requirement of 'being regarded as having such an impairment' if the individual establishes that he or she has been subjected to an action prohibited under this chapter because of an actual or perceived physical or mental impairment whether or not the impairment limits or is perceived to limit a major life activity."[27]

The Equal Employment Opportunity Commission (EEOC) has interpreted section 12102(3) to include individuals who are subjected to differential treatment because of the perceptions of others. The EEOC publication provides the following:

(d) Persons Who Are Substantially Limited as a Result of Others' Attitudes—This subpart covers individuals who have stigmatic conditions that constitute physical or mental impairments but that do not by themselves substantially limit a major life activity. The impairments become substantially limiting only because of the negative reactions of others toward the impairments. For example, a person who has experienced severe burns may have an impairment that is substantially limiting solely because of the attitudes of others. Similarly, a person who has a cosmetic disfigurement may be continuously refused employment because of employers' fears about the negative reactions of co-workers or clients. These persons would be covered under the third part of the definition of the term "disability."[28]

Individuals with an intersex condition may suffer discrimination in a number of areas protected under the ADA. They may be subjected to differential treatment in the provision of health care, adoption proceedings,[29] and schooling.[30] The area that is likely to have the greatest impact on children with an intersex condition is in the provision of health services. Infants with an intersex condition frequently are subjected to medically unnecessary cosmetic surgeries that may impair their ability to engage in satisfactory sex, affect continence, render them infertile, and inflict severe psychological trauma. These surgeries, which have not been proven to be beneficial, are being performed on healthy children with an intersex condition even though procedures that pose the same risks would not be performed on children who do not have an intersex condition. Therefore, it could be argued that subjecting these children to potentially disabling invasive surgeries because they are "perceived as being impaired" constitutes disability discrimination.

### State Disability Laws

In addition to federal disability laws, disability claims could also be based on violations of state laws. The recent report published by the Washington Protection and Advocacy System (WPAS)[31] involving the treatment of "Ashley X" could provide the basis for a claim brought on behalf of children with an intersex condition.[32] Ashley was born with profound developmental disabilities. Doctors predicted that her mental capacity would never develop beyond that of an infant. At the age of six, Ashley could not sit up, ambulate, or use speech. She was dependent on a gastronomy tube for her nutrition. Despite her disabilities, Ashley was an integral member of the family and her parents wanted to continue to care for her at home. They did not want her care to be put in the hands of strangers. When Ashley began to display signs of early puberty, her parents became concerned that they would not be able to care for her as she continued to grow and mature.[33]

Ashley's parents and doctors developed a plan to stunt Ashley's growth and to repress her sexual development by having doctors perform a hysterectomy to prevent menstruation and a mastectomy to prevent development of breast tissue. They also planned to administer estrogen to prevent her from reaching her projected adult height and weight. The goal of these treatments was to allow Ashley's parents to continue her home care and to avoid potential complications of early puberty.[34]

Because of the extensive nature of the planned intervention, Ashley's physicians sought guidance from the hospital ethics committee. The committee approved the proposed treatment and advised the parents to obtain legal advice regarding the procedures that would lead to sterility. The parents hired an attorney to advise them about whether they required a court order before they could initiate the procedures. Their attorney advised them that they did not need a court order, so they proceeded without one. When news about Ashley's treatment became public, disability rights groups protested. They argued that the motivation for the treatment may have been to benefit Ashley's parents, rather than Ashley, and that the treatment was dehumanizing.[35]

Ashley's treatment was investigated by the WPAS, the federally mandated protection and advocacy agency for the state of Washington. The WPAS has legal authority under federal law to investigate allegations of mistreatment of persons with a disability within the state of Washington.[36] The WPAS determined that Ashley's treatment violated her constitutional and common law rights and was a direct violation of Washington law. The agency ruled that parents and doctors cannot agree to sterilize children without a court order. Such a procedure requires a court finding that the sterilization is in the child's best interests. The court order must be issued after an adversarial proceeding in which the child's interests must be zealously represented by a disinterested third party.[37]

The WPAS did not limit its holding to the procedures that resulted in sterilization. It also held that Ashley's constitutional liberty and privacy rights were affected by any procedures that were invasive and irreversible. Therefore, it held that the removal of Ashley's breast buds and the administration of high doses of hormones also implicated her constitutional right to liberty and privacy and should be subjected to court review.[38]

The issues considered by the WPAS in the Ashley X case apply with equal, if not greater, force to surgeries performed on infants with an intersex condition. Some of these surgeries have the potential for analogous invasions of constitutionally protected liberty and privacy rights. Surgeries performed on infants with an intersex condition should be subjected to even greater scrutiny than the treatment of a child with developmental disabilities. A person with developmental disabilities as severe as Ashley's will never be able to understand and consent to the treatments administered. She will always require her parents' care and will never be in a position where she will be able to make these decisions for herself. In contrast, children with an intersex condition will eventually reach an age when they are able to provide their own informed consent. Therefore, performing highly invasive and potentially life altering surgeries on infants with an intersex condition on the basis of parental consent alone is less justifiable. Given the fact that children with an intersex condition will eventually be able to make this decision on their own, a stronger argument for nonintervention during infancy exists.[39]

*Some Intersex Activists Oppose the Use of a Disability Framework*

Although disability discrimination statutes might prove to be a fruitful avenue to address the goals of the intersex movement, many people with an intersex condition object to the use of a disability model. A recent transition in the terminology used in this area illustrates this unease. Most physicians and many intersex activists (especially in the United States) have rejected the term *intersex* in favor of the term *disorders of sex development* (*DSD*). Although *DSD* is becoming the norm in many medical publications, this change in terminology has not met with universal support.

Some activists recognize the problems inherent in the use of the term *intersex*. They acknowledge that the term *intersex* may lead to confusion and stigma because it implies that people with an intersex condition are neither male nor female but are instead between the sexes. They reject the substitution of the term *disorder*, however, because of the stigma associated in our society with people who are disabled or disordered. Some prefer that the "D" in *DSD* represent "difference" rather than "disorder," while others have advocated for the use of *VRD* to represent "variations of reproductive development," because these terms avoid the stigmatization associated with the word *disorder*.[40] Organisation Intersex International (OII) is critical of the term *DSD* because it increases medical pathologization and the stigma associated with the term *disorder*.[41]

This aversion to the term *disorder* stems from the twentieth-century medical model under which people with disabilities tend to evoke pity. Opponents of the DSD terminology fear that the label *disorder* will result in people with a DSD being viewed as not fully functional. They are concerned that the societal response will be to "cure" their disorder by medically modifying their bodies and rehabilitating them so that they can become as "normal" as possible. Opponents of the term *DSD* fear that the label will perpetuate stigma and social prejudice because those with disabilities are viewed as inferior to those who are "normal."

Disability rights groups, using critical disability theory, have challenged this framework. Instead of focusing on the individual who is different, critical disability theorists focus on the barriers society has created to block the full participation of people with disabilities. Under this view, disabilities are only impairments if society is not structured so that those with disabilities are able to participate fully. The classic example used to illustrate this alternative vision is a person in a wheelchair. Those who cannot walk are unable to participate fully in a society that provides only stairs and escalators and not ramps and elevators. In a world in which all buildings are accessible to those in wheelchairs, those who cannot walk are not disabled from full participation. By shifting the focus away from the bodies of disabled people and onto societal structures that inhibit full participation, critical disability theorists argue that body differences potentially can become no more significant than hair or eye color.[42]

Most people with an intersex condition are able to participate fully in society and do not consider themselves "disabled" or "disordered." Critical disability theorists assert that social institutions that use bright-line tests to distinguish male bodies from female bodies and that view all bodies that do not meet these binary tests as abnormal, create the disability. The societal disposition to divide bodies into normal and abnormal and to privilege some types of bodies over others renders people with an intersex condition "disabled." As intersex activist Esther Morris has written, "Being born without a vagina was not my problem; having to get one was the real problem."[43]

Although some intersex activists oppose the use of a disability model, disability laws can be effective tools in the fight against discrimination because of their extensive coverage and liberal interpretation. People with an intersex condition who suffer discrimination in the provision of health care or other protected areas under disability laws could assert that they have been subjected to differential treatment because of their perceived disability. Intersex activists could use disability laws and join the battle with others in the critical disability movement who are working to end the shame and stigma associated with disabilities and disorders. If that goal is achieved, people with a DSD/intersex condition would no longer require disability laws to protect them because the perception that they are impaired and in need of fixing will have been successfully debunked.

### Statutes Prohibiting Sex Discrimination

People with an intersex condition could also be protected under laws prohibiting discrimination because of "sex." Federal, state, and local laws prohibit sex discrimination in a number of settings, including employment, housing, education, and health care.[44] Although hundreds of statutes and administrative regulations prohibit discrimination because of "sex," the meaning of the term *sex* in these legislative acts is far from clear. When laws prohibiting sex discrimination were first adopted, courts tended to rule that the purpose of the legislation was to provide equal opportunities for women and men. The typical early successful sex discrimination cases involved men or women who were treated differently because of their biologic sex. For example, early decisions invalidated employer rules providing that only men could be airline pilots and only women could be flight attendants.

During the first three decades after sex discrimination prohibitions were enacted in 1964, courts generally refused to expand the meaning of the term *sex* beyond this simple approach. The statutory ban against sex discrimination did not protect people from discriminatory treatment based on their being a man or a woman who failed to conform to gender role stereotypes,[45] a pregnant woman,[46] gay or lesbian,[47] or a transsexual.[48]

In addition, one court did not allow a person with an intersex condition to recover under a statute prohibiting discrimination because of sex. Only one reported case addresses whether a person with an intersex condition can recover under a statute prohibiting sex discrimination. In 1987 in *Wood v. C.G. Studios*, a federal district court considered a case in which an employer terminated an employee after he learned that she had undergone surgery to "correct" her "hermaphroditic" condition before she began her employment. The court refused to treat the employer's actions as sex discrimination. It analyzed the history of the act and found that the purpose of the legislation was to provide equal employment opportunities to women. The court ruled that the statute was not intended to remedy discrimination against individuals because they have undergone gender corrective surgery. Therefore, the court limited the meaning of the word *sex* in the statute to what it considered its "plain meaning" and held that sex discrimination prohibitions do not encompass discrimination against "hermaphrodites" because of their intersex status.[49]

During the 1990s, this limited vision of sex discrimination began to dissolve in large part due to the feminist and LGBT movements and feminist and queer theorists, who helped to educate society and the judiciary about the complex nature of sex discrimination. They helped courts develop a more nuanced understanding of the meaning and harm of sex discrimination. This new conceptualization of sex discrimination could potentially form the basis for a legal argument by a person with an intersex condition.

The major case expanding the meaning of the word *sex* was the U.S. Supreme Court's 1989 ruling in *Price Waterhouse v. Hopkins*.[50] In this case, an accounting firm denied a partnership to Hopkins, not because she was biologically a woman but because she failed to meet the partners' stereotyped expectations of how a woman should behave. The partners implied that her failure to conform to stereotypes of femininity blocked her path to partnership. Specifically, Hopkins was told that she overcompensated for being a woman and was "too macho."[51] She was advised to stop using profanity, to take a class at charm school, and to "walk more femininely, talk more femininely, wear make-up, have her hair styled, and wear jewelry."[52] The Supreme Court ruled that discrimination against a woman because she failed to conform to societal stereotypes of femininity constituted discrimination because of sex.

The Court's acceptance of sex stereotyping as a form of impermissible sex discrimination reflects a more sophisticated understanding of the harms of sex based discriminatory conduct. Based on the *Price Waterhouse* decision, individuals who suffer discrimination because they fail to conform to sex related stereotypes have been able to prove that they have suffered impermissible sex discrimination.

During the past decade, a number of groups that were consistently excluded from sex discrimination coverage before *Price Waterhouse* have been allowed to state a cause of action if their claim is appropriately framed as gender nonconformity or sex stereotyping discrimination. A number of courts have embraced the concept that gender role performance, sexual orientation, and gender identity are part of a person's "sex." These courts have prohibited discrimination against people whose gender roles, sexual practices, and gender identities fail to conform to societal norms.

*Gender Role Performance*

Many men and women suffer from discrimination when they opt to fulfill roles that do not comport with societal stereotypes about appropriate roles for males and females. Although courts originally ruled that sex discrimination statutes did not encompass discrimination based on gender role stereotyping, recently some courts have allowed recovery based on this theory.

New mothers who have suffered an adverse employment decision because their employers believed that they would fail to conform to the norm of the ideal worker have successfully maintained cases based on gender role stereotyping.[53] For example, in *Back v. Hastings*, school psychologist Elena Back stated a sex stereotyping claim when she was denied tenure. Back took a maternity leave after she gave birth. She returned to work and was subsequently denied tenure. During the review process, her supervisors made comments questioning her ability as a new mother to devote herself to her job. The court held that these statements were evidence of sex stereotyping discrimination because they indicated a presumption that being a mother is incompatible with being an effective worker.[54]

Similarly, some courts have granted recovery to men who suffered discrimination because they failed to conform to the norm of a male "breadwinner" when they sought time off for family care responsibilities.[55] For example, Maryland State Trooper Howard Kevin Knussman alleged that he suffered sex discrimination when his employer refused to grant him paid leave to care for his wife and newborn child. His wife suffered medical problems during the pregnancy and after the birth. Knussman sought paid leave under a gender neutral statute granting "nurturing leave" for the care of a newborn. The court ruled that the employer engaged in unlawful sex discrimination because its decision to deny Knussman paid leave was based on stereotypes about the proper role of men and women.[56]

### Sexual Practices

Gays and lesbians, who before *Price Waterhouse* consistently lost their sex discrimination claims, are now sometimes successful in convincing courts that they are victims of sex discrimination when they are harassed or otherwise discriminated against because they fail to conform to sex and gender norms.[57] For example, Medina Rene, an openly gay male butler at the MGM Grand Hotel in Las Vegas, was able to prove he had suffered sex discrimination at the hands of the other butlers. All the other butlers, as well as Rene's supervisor, were male. Rene testified that during his two years at the MGM, he had been continuously subjected to harassment by his supervisor and fellow butlers. The harassers whistled and blew kisses at Rene; they called him "sweetheart" and "muñeca" (Spanish for "doll"); they gave him sexually oriented "joke" gifts; and they forced him to look at pictures of naked men having sex. He was also subjected to physical harassment of a sexual nature. Rene stated that the other employees would treat him as they would treat a woman because they knew he was gay. The court held that the fact that he was treated "like a woman" constitutes ample evidence of gender stereotyping.[58]

### Gender Identity

A string of cases beginning in the 1970s denied transsexuals the ability to state a sex discrimination claim. A number of recent decisions, however, have held that sex discrimination prohibitions protect transsexual plaintiffs.[59] For example, firefighting lieutenant Jimmie L. Smith had worked for seven years in the Salem, Ohio, fire department without any negative incidents. After Lieutenant Smith began his transition to becoming a woman, his co-workers began questioning him about his appearance and commenting that his looks and mannerisms were not "masculine enough." Smith decided to notify his supervisor that he was in the process of transitioning and that he would eventually undergo a complete physical transformation and become a woman. After he disclosed his transsexual status, his employer instituted a plan to fire him. The court held that Smith had been discriminated against under the *Price Waterhouse* sexual stereotyping theory because his treatment was based on his failure to conform to stereotypes of how men should look and behave. A federal circuit court ruled that the earlier cases that had denied the ability of transsexuals to recover for sex discrimination were "eviscerated" by the 1989 holding in *Price Waterhouse*.[60]

The ability of transsexuals to recover under a sex discrimination theory expanded dramatically after the 2008 federal district court ruling in *Schroer v. Billington*.[61] Diane Schroer, a male-to-female transsexual, applied for a position with the research division of the Library of Congress as a terrorism specialist providing expert policy analysis to Congress. When she applied for the job, she had not yet transitioned, so she used her legal male name, David, on the application and she attended the interview in male clothing. She received the highest score of the eighteen candidates and she was offered the job. Diane accepted the position, but before she began work, she notified the person in charge of hiring that she would begin work as a female. The job offer was revoked and Diane sued.

The court found that the Library of Congress had engaged in unlawful sex discrimination for two reasons. First, the court found that the Library of Congress engaged in sex stereotyping discrimination that was found actionable in *Price Waterhouse*. The court concluded that different comments by the employer indicated that Diane was viewed as an insufficiently masculine man, an insufficiently feminine woman, or an inherently gender nonconforming transsexual.[62] The court stated, "The Library was enthusiastic about hiring David Schroer—until she disclosed her transsexuality. The Library revoked the offer when it learned that a man named David intended to become, legally, culturally, and physically, a woman named Diane. This was discrimination 'because of . . . sex.'"[63]

More important, the court also found that Diane could recover under a straightforward sex discrimination theory and she did not need to rely on the gender nonconformity approach. The court ruled that people who "change" their sex and suffer discrimination because of the transition have suffered sex discrimination. The court continued,

> Imagine that an employee is fired because she converts from Christianity to Judaism. Imagine too that her employer testifies that he harbors no bias toward either Christians or Jews but only "converts." That would be a clear case of discrimination "because of religion." No court would take seriously the notion that "converts" are not covered by the statute. Discrimination "because of religion" easily encompasses discrimination because of a change of religion. But in cases where the plaintiff has changed her

sex, and faces discrimination because of the decision to stop presenting as a man and to start appearing as a woman, courts have traditionally carved such persons out of the statute by concluding that "transsexuality" is unprotected by Title VII. In other words, courts have allowed their focus on the label "transsexual" to blind them to the statutory language itself.[64]

The *Schroer* court abandoned the historical approach that limited recovery in sex discrimination cases to men who were treated differently from women and women who were treated differently from men. It specifically rejected cases that had denied transsexuals the ability to state a sex discrimination claim because of their failure to fit into the male/female sex binary.

### Sex Discrimination Claims on Behalf of People with an Intersex Condition

Based on these recent cases, a sex discrimination framework could prove to be a successful avenue to protect the rights of people with an intersex condition in jurisdictions adopting a more nuanced understanding and expanded definition of sex discrimination.

The sex stereotyping theory could apply if doctors continue to alter the bodies of infants born with an intersex condition so that they conform to sex and gender norms. For example, if the surgical plan prioritizes the appearance of a female's genitalia over her ability to experience sexual pleasure, a court could conclude that the intervention is based on the stereotype that a feminine appearance is more important to a woman than is the ability to orgasm. In addition, under the court's holding in *Schroer*, people with an intersex condition who are treated differently from people who do not have an intersex condition could potentially state a sex discrimination claim. The same reasoning that the *Schroer* court applied to transsexuals could be applied to people with an intersex condition. If infants with an intersex condition are subjected to genital surgery because doctors decide that they are not sufficiently male or female, they have arguably been subjected to differential treatment because of their intersex status.

In addition, if people suffer an adverse employment decision because of their intersex condition, they could potentially assert that such discrimination was because of their sex. Although the federal district court ruled in *Wood v. C.G. Studios*[65] that such a claim did not constitute sex discrimination, if a similar case were brought today, the likelihood of success is high. The *Price Waterhouse* and *Schroer* decisions and other, more recent cases protecting sex and gender nonconforming men and women could provide the basis for determining that such an action constitutes discrimination because of sex.

## The Patient Protection and Affordable Care Act

The Patient Protection and Affordable Care Act, which was signed into law in 2010, may provide the strongest basis for a discrimination claim related to the provision of health care.[66] Although the act does not specifically address the medical treatment of people with an intersex condition, it prohibits both sex and disability discrimination in the provision of health care.[67] To the extent that infants with an intersex condition are subjected to differential treatment based on sex or perceived disability, they may be entitled to recover under this act.

The Patient Protection and Affordable Care Act provides,

[A]n individual shall not, on the ground prohibited under title VI of the Civil Rights Act of 1964 (42 U.S.C. 2000d et seq.), title IX of the Education Amendments of 1972 (20 U.S.C. 1681 et seq.), the Age Discrimination Act of 1975 (42 U.S.C. 6101 et seq.), or section 504 of the Rehabilitation Act of 1973 (29 U.S.C. 794), be excluded from participation in, be denied the benefits of, or be subjected to discrimination under, any health program or activity, any part of which is receiving Federal financial assistance, including credits, subsidies, or contracts of insurance, or under any program or activity that is administered by an Executive Agency or any entity established under this title (or amendments).[68]

Therefore, to the extent that a hospital is subject to this act, it could be in violation if its medical treatment of infants born with an intersex condition is considered sex or disability discrimination.

## Specific Legislation Protecting People with an Intersex Condition

Because some courts may be unwilling to apply sex discrimination prohibitions to claims brought by people with an intersex condition, the intersex movement may want to encourage legislatures to adopt statutes that specifically protect the intersex community. Some states and cities have expanded their antidiscrimination protections to include discrimination because of sexual orientation or gender identity. Eight states (Connecticut, Delaware, Maryland, Massachusetts, Nevada, New Hampshire, New York, and Wisconsin) have adopted statutes prohibiting discrimination based on sexual orientation.[69] An additional fourteen jurisdictions (California, Colorado, the District of Columbia, Hawaii, Illinois, Iowa, Maine, Minnesota, New Jersey,

New Mexico, Oregon, Rhode Island, Vermont, and Washington) prohibit discrimination based on sexual orientation and gender identity or expression.[70] On numerous occasions, Congress has considered and failed to pass the Employment Nondiscrimination Act (ENDA), which would have prohibited sexual orientation discrimination in employment.[71] Antidiscrimination statutes that prohibit discrimination based on sex, sexual orientation, and gender identity/expression could be interpreted to include people with an intersex condition. Protection would be more certain, however, if statutes are adopted that specifically protect people with an intersex condition from discrimination.

In conclusion, the intersex movement could convince legal institutions, including administrative agencies, legislatures, and courts, to protect them from discriminatory practices in a number of ways. The most effective method would be to persuade legislatures to adopt laws that specifically address the needs of the intersex community. Given the small size of the intersex community and the limited funds available to intersex advocacy groups, it is unlikely that the lobbying efforts to pass such legislation would be successful. Alternatively, current statutes prohibiting disability and sex discrimination could provide persuasive frameworks to protect adults with an intersex condition from discriminatory actions as well as to provide enhanced safeguards when a decision to surgically alter the genitalia of an infant with an intersex condition is being contemplated. Regardless of the legal advocacy path the intersex movement chooses to follow, the likelihood of success will be enhanced if this relatively small and underfunded movement is able to form effective alliances with other subordinated groups suffering from similar types of discriminatory practices. The potential for forming these mutually beneficial alliances is explored in the concluding chapter.

# Conclusion

The current protocol for the treatment of intersex conditions is based on sex, gender, sexual orientation, and disability presumptions about which bodies qualify as "normal." Current belief systems require that children raised as girls have female appearing genitalia, including a clitoris that is not "too large" and a vagina that is capable of accommodating a penis. These norms also require that children who are going to be raised as boys have a penis that is capable of penetrating a vagina and allows the male to stand while urinating. Bodies that fail to comport to these standards are often perceived as nonconforming, disabled, and in need of repair. Typically, the "fix" is to subject these children to surgeries that have in some cases led to lifelong physical complications and psychological harm.

In a relatively short time, intersex activists have increased public awareness about issues facing the intersex community and have commenced a productive dialogue with medical practitioners. Although these educational efforts have started to shift some practices, the change is neither swift nor universal and many life altering surgeries are still being performed.[1]

The intersex movement is situated at a critical crossroads. The movement is still in the process of (1) developing effective strategies to accomplish its goals, (2) determining who should be considered part of the movement, and (3) deciding whether to form alliances with other progressive movements with similar concerns. These issues are not unique to the intersex movement. All social justice movements have struggled with issues relating to inclusion and exclusion, priority setting, and developing strategies. These types of conflicts are part of the process of building a strong movement.

Because a combination of normative assumptions about sex, gender, sexual orientation, and disabled bodies drive current medical practices, the intersex movement could adopt a number of legal strategies and form a variety of alliances to accomplish its goal of ensuring that decisions about the appropriate treatment for infants with an intersex condition are made under optimal circumstances. As intersex advocates develop their tactics, they need to recognize that as more people with an intersex condition enter adulthood with genitalia that do not comport with the male/female binary norm, the type of discrimination currently directed against transsexuals may also be experienced by people with an intersex condition. Therefore, as the movement develops its strategies, it must be cognizant of how the frameworks it adopts could affect adults with an intersex condition.

## Using the Law to Protect People with an Intersex Condition

The law's focus on rights, equality, and justice can serve as a powerful tool to sway public opinion and to accomplish societal reform.[2] Beginning with the civil rights movement in the 1960s, progressive social justice movements increasingly have used legal advocacy to accomplish societal change. For example, the LGBT movement successfully advocated for and achieved decriminalization of sexual practices, protection under some antidiscrimination statutes, and legal recognition of LGBT family relationships in some jurisdictions. Blacks and other racial minorities achieved access to opportunities that had been denied to them on the basis of their race and skin color. Women effectively advanced legal arguments that opened the doors to equal employment opportunities and provided greater protection and rights in their family relationships. Although Blacks, LGBTs, and women have not yet attained economic and social equality, legal reform has played a significant role in altering societal perceptions and advancing these movements toward their goals.

Thus far, the intersex movement has focused most of its efforts on extra-legal strategies. Legal challenges can provide an additional effective tool to improve the treatment of infants and adults with an intersex condition. Because the current medical protocol for the treatment of infants with an intersex condition may infringe on a child's right to bodily autonomy, a fundamental interest subject to legal protection, legal institutions may be able to play a constructive role in ensuring that the infant's rights are adequately protected. In addition, legal challenges to sex classification systems may be the most effective way to ensure that people with an intersex condition are protected from discrimination relating to their right to marry, to have their identity documents reflect their self-identity, and to use sex segregated public facilities of their choice.

No current laws specifically address the treatment of people with an intersex condition. A successful lobbying campaign would require significant financial and human resources. Therefore, in the short run it may be more realistic for intersex advocates to persuade legal institutions to apply existing disability and sex discrimination statutes to their claims. Because most people with an intersex condition are not actually impaired and are able to participate fully in all life activities, they could not state a claim for discrimination based on an actual disability. Potentially, they could persuade a court that infants with an intersex condition are subjected to differential treatment because they are perceived as impaired. The dominant medical protocol supports medically unnecessary cosmetic genital surgery to "fix" a perceived disability, without any proof that the condition is actually disabling. Therefore, courts could find that the current medical protocol violates the ADA and other disability discrimination statutes under the "perceived as impaired" provisions.

Stating a claim under a sex discrimination statute requires that courts develop a more nuanced understanding of the harms of discrimination based on sex stereotyping. Thus far, only one court has addressed whether a statute prohibiting sex discrimination protects an employee with an intersex condition from discrimination. That court interpreted the term *sex* narrowly and ruled that the statute did not apply.[3] The rulings in more recent cases involving transsexuals and other nonconforming men and women indicate that many (but not all) courts are expanding recovery to prohibit discrimination based on sex stereotyping. Therefore, intersex advocates will need to persuade courts that sex discrimination incorporates discrimination against people on the basis of their intersex status.

Convincing courts or legislatures to impose greater oversight of infant genital surgeries may also require decision makers to prioritize the child's right to autonomy over parental rights to make decisions on behalf of their minor children. Under current statutes and court decisions governing the sterilization of developmentally disabled people, medical procedures that result in sterilization can only be performed under a court order. These statutes should also apply to sterilizations of infants with an intersex condition. In contrast, parental decisions regarding medical procedures for their children that do not result in sterilization are typically granted deference. Therefore, courts are unlikely to completely ban all cosmetic genital surgeries that do not result in sterilization. Given the life altering nature of these surgeries, a reasonable approach would be to convince courts and legislatures to impose safeguards in the form of enhanced informed consent procedures or review and approval by an independent decision maker.

## Forming Effective Alliances to Support Legal Challenges

Disability rights groups and organizations focused on ending discrimination based on sex, gender, sexual orientation, and gender identity could play a critical role in advancing the legal claims of people with an intersex condition. These organizations have more members, greater access to resources, and more extensive connections with lawmakers than does the nascent intersex movement. Forming and maintaining alliances with these social justice movements may not be easy, but these alliances could potentially enhance the likelihood that the intersex movement will accomplish its goals.

Building a strong movement requires that intersex advocates develop effective strategies to negotiate the pitfalls that have plagued other social justice movements. Conflicts between movement members and among organizations that share related goals have derailed a number of social justice movements and have hampered progress in others.

Intragroup disputes have arisen in a number of progressive movements about who qualifies as a member and what issues should be prioritized. For example, early second-wave feminists rejected transwomen from membership. They also failed to prioritize the issues confronting lesbian women, women of color, and women of lower socioeconomic status. Similarly, at the start of the gay and lesbian movement, many of the major organizations rejected the inclusion of transsexuals and ignored the special issues they confronted. In addition, bisexuals who wanted to join the gay movement were initially criticized for their willingness to engage in sex with a person of the opposite sex.

Forming alliances among different social justice movements has also been problematic. Sometimes, members of marginalized groups whose missions include promoting equality for all subordinated individuals have played a critical role in actually furthering discrimination against other oppressed groups. Often, progressive movements have embraced essentialist viewpoints and viewed other groups as oppositional and in competition, rather than as potential allies. Navigating these differences requires a deeper understanding of problems that have plagued most social justice movements, in which narrow definitions of group interests and "not our problem" attitudes fail to recognize the multidimensional and complex nature of subordination.[4]

Scholars studying social justice movements suggest that progressive movements abandon traditional single-issue identity politics and move toward an antisubordination framework that focuses on structural systems of inequality. They recognize that articulating a valid legal claim often requires an individual to rely on identity categories, but they assert that discrete identity categories often are inadequate to effectively address complex systems of subordination. Therefore, they encourage progressive social justice movements to recognize the connections between different identity groups and to form coalitions to jointly pursue societal reform.[5]

One key to building effective coalitions is to develop strategies that address common problems, while recognizing that not all differences can always be overcome.[6] This process requires individuals to respect the fact that different organizations and individual members within an organization may have diverse priorities. When agendas diverge, it is important not to advance arguments that have the potential to harm others and to attempt to be as inclusive as possible.[7]

In addition, progressive movements are sometimes hamstrung when individuals within the movement subscribe to a hierarchical notion of oppression. This view promotes the belief that some individuals' needs should be prioritized because the harm they have endured is of a greater magnitude.

> [D]ifference is almost always translated into us/them politics, which in turn provides a never-ending list of possible ways to place people into dominant/subordinate statuses. . . . Given the ever-increasing number of acknowledged forms of inequality and the tendency among identity-based groups to rank one form of oppression as more important than another, attempts at coalition building, even among subordinate groups, often appear impossible.[8]

Forging meaningful coalitions among groups with related but differing priorities requires the development of dynamic and flexible alliances. Diverse individuals forming these coalitions must recognize their shared goals and negotiate their differences. If potential allies fail to understand the intersecting oppression suffered by all marginalized groups, they will be unable to challenge the core reasons maintaining their subordinated status.[9]

Some of the issues that have hampered progress in other social justice movements have already caused conflict in the intersex movement. To enhance the building of a strong and effective movement, intersex advocates need to address differences that have arisen among the movement's members and between the intersex movement and other social justice movements.

Addressing the conflicts that have developed within the movement requires advocates to be sensitive to the unique experiences and perspectives of its diverse membership. Issues relating to language and inclusion/exclusion have led to heated debates that have the potential to fracture the movement's progress. For example, using the terms *intersex* and *DSD* have both led to problems. Some parents who do not want their child labeled *intersex* have rejected inclusion in the movement and distanced themselves from intersex activist organizations. In the same manner, the move to the DSD terminology also caused protests by some intersex advocates. The change to the DSD terminology occurred rapidly and without a widespread vetting before the modification was adopted. A number of people with an intersex condition resented having the label *disorder* applied to them. The intersex community also has been hampered by disagreements about who qualifies as a member of the community. When the intersex movement began, some intersex activists who had been subjected to surgical modification differentiated themselves from persons with an intersex condition who had not undergone invasive medical treatments. Some who wanted to join the community were turned away as "intersex wannabes."[10] As the movement develops, it needs to be sensitive to the diverse experiences, needs, and viewpoints of its members.

Intersex community members also have disagreed about the benefits of forming alliances with other marginalized groups. Although the disability rights movement and LGBT groups could play a critical role in helping the intersex movement, some intersex advocates reject an association with these organizations. Many people with an intersex condition do not view themselves as disabled or disordered and do not want to be part of a "disability" movement. The critical disability movement, however, may provide the most effective model for mounting challenges to current medical practices that prioritize "fixing" bodies rather than teaching society to accommodate differences. The critical disability movement could assist the intersex movement in its efforts to enhance societal acceptance of people whose genitalia and reproductive systems are different. Other intersex activists reject the idea of forming alliances with LGBT groups. Some intersex advocates assert that they do not want to be associated with an identity movement, especially a "queer" movement, because they do not self-identify as sex or gender nonconformists and they fear that such an association will lead to increased surgeries on infants with an intersex condition.

The intersex community is small and has access to limited resources. Therefore, the movement could benefit from building alliances and developing strategies in conjunction with more well established advocacy groups. To form effective alliances requires the movement to address these concerns among its members. Building alliances with other progressive movements will require the intersex movement to educate other social justice movements about potential areas where their interests converge and diverge.

Intersex activists could help feminists understand how the goals of the two communities intersect. The feminist movement has worked to eliminate discrimination based on sex and gender stereotypes and to protect women's rights to bodily autonomy, especially in areas involving reproductive and sexual freedom. Thus far, the feminist movement has not recognized that excluding intersex issues from the feminist agenda has the potential to perpetuate sex discrimination and to further the subordination of women. As feminists learn more about the rationales supporting surgical alteration of infants with an intersex condition, they may realize that some current medical practices involve concerns that are at the heart of most feminist agendas. First, surgical alteration of the genitalia and reproductive systems of girls with an intersex condition threaten women's rights to privacy, liberty, and bodily autonomy because these irreversible, life altering procedures are being performed without the girl's consent. Second, the protocols themselves are based on medically created gender norms about which penises are too small and which clitorises are too large. Finally, these practices are based on false stereotypes about women because they assume that all females will emphasize genital appearance over sexual pleasure and will have the desire to engage in traditional heterosexual intercourse over other forms of sexual pleasure.

In addition to concerns about cosmetic genital surgery, feminists should also be concerned about other medical practices related to the treatment of ambiguous genitalia. To prevent the potential masculinization of fetuses that may have congenital adrenal hyperplasia (CAH), some doctors are administering a powerful drug to pregnant mothers who have an increased chance of carrying a CAH baby. As discussed in more detail in chapter 9, researchers advocating use of this drug have noted that a side benefit may be the enhancement of feminine thinking and behavior in the child. The use of drugs to create girls who are interested in playing with dolls and raising babies should be of grave concern to feminists.

Working with the LGBT community requires that intersex advocates educate LGBT groups about where their interests and goals diverge. Unlike feminists, LGBT organizations have recognized that discrimination against people with an intersex condition is generated in part by homophobia. Thus, many LGBT organizations have added an "I" to their moniker. Most of these organizations, however, have not taken the steps necessary to fully understand how the critical issues facing the intersex community differ from the top LGBT agenda items. If LGBT organizations decide to add the "I" to their names, they need to focus their resources on addressing the priorities of the intersex movement. These LGBT organizations need to be sensitive to the fact that although some individuals with an intersex condition view themselves as gender nonconformists and identify with a "queer" identity movement that challenges sex, gender, and sexual orientation norms, not all think of their intersex condition as a part of their identity and they may not want to be incorporated into a queer identity movement.

Furthermore, gays and lesbians, and especially transsexuals, need to be educated about how their use of intersex rhetoric may negatively affect members of the intersex community. Gays, lesbians, and transsexuals have argued that the existence of intersexuality supports their claim that sexual orientation and transsexuality may also have a biological basis. When they make this argument, LGBT advocates need to consider how associating intersexuality with sexual orientation and gender identity may have the potential to increase the number of cosmetic genital surgeries on infants with an intersex condition. When parents are deciding whether to have their child surgically altered, many parents consider whether it will decrease the likelihood that their child will be gay or a transsexual. Therefore, before LGBT organizations add the "I" to their name or rely on intersex rhetoric, they must carefully assess whether doing so will serve to help accomplish the intersex movement's primary goals or whether it might inadvertently lead to more surgeries on infants with an intersex condition.

Perhaps most important, the intersex movement must recognize that as it turns to legal strategies to accomplish its goals, legislators and courts will inevitably draw comparisons between persons with an intersex condition and transsexuals. The law tends to be a blunt instrument for accomplishing change. It often tends to ignore subtle and not so subtle differences when it creates rules that are designed to apply to a large, diverse society. The conflation of intersexuality and transsexuality in legal decisions has already occurred in a number of areas. Intersex persons and transsexuals have been subjected to the same types of rules in marriage cases,[11] requests for modification of sex designation,[12] and decisions about sex-segregated housing.[13] Therefore, both movements need to be aware of how their legal advocacy strategies may assist or harm each other. Although the current primary concerns of the intersex and transsexual movements are distinct, both movements could benefit in the long run from developing coordinated legal strategies.

•   •   •

Sex matters. It matters socially, politically, and legally. Most important, it matters to the people who are harmed by society's failure to protect them from discriminatory practices based on sex stereotypes. We should not continue to leave decisions about the treatment of people with an intersex condition solely to medical practitioners. In areas involving sex and gender, science is in its infancy and has engaged in a number of harmful practices based on unsupported theories that later proved to be incorrect.

No conclusive studies have been conducted to determine whether the current medical treatment protocol, which continues to support surgical alteration of "atypical" appearing genitalia, is beneficial. Given this uncertainty and the critical constitutionally protected rights at stake, legal institutions should take a more active role in ensuring that the rights of people with an intersex condition are protected.

Enhancing the quality of life for people with an intersex condition requires a multipronged attack. The productive dialogues that have started with medical experts need to be enhanced. Society needs to be educated about the problems surrounding the current treatment of intersex conditions. Legal arguments need to be developed to ensure that the rights of people with an intersex condition are protected. Most important, people interested in enhancing the lives of marginalized groups need to work together to develop mutually beneficial strategies. Activists concerned with ending subordination and marginalization of people whose bodies or activities do not fit societal norms can play a critical role in this process.

# Appendix

## Common Intersex/DSD Conditions

| | Chromosomes | Gonads | Genitalia | Internal sex | Hormones | Phenotype | Assigned sex | Self-identification |
|---|---|---|---|---|---|---|---|---|
| Klinefelter syndrome | O[1] | M | M[2] | M | M[3] | O[4] | M | M[5] |
| Turner syndrome | O[6] | O[7] | F | F | O[8] | F[9] | F | F |
| Swyer syndrome | M | O[7] | F | F | O[8] | F[9] | F | F |
| CAIS | M | M | F | O[10] | O[11] | F | F | F |
| PAIS | M | M | V | V[12] | O[11] | F | V | V |
| 5 alpha reductase deficiency | M | M | O[13] | M | M | O[14] | O[15] | V |
| Virilizing CAH | F | F | O[16] | F | O[17] | O[18] | F[19] | V |

M = Male   F = Female   O = Other   V = Varies

1. Individuals with Klinefelter syndrome have two or more X chromosomes in addition to a Y chromosome.
2. The external genitalia are typically smaller than in unaffected males.
3. Hormones are typically at low levels.
4. Phenotype is male at birth, but at the onset of puberty, breasts may swell.
5. Primarily male but may vary.
6. Individuals with Turner syndrome have an XO chromosomal pattern.
7. The gonads are "streak" gonads and are unformed and nonfunctioning.
8. Because the gonads are incomplete, the exposure to hormones is reduced.
9. At puberty, little breast enlargement occurs.
10. No internal reproductive organs are created, and the vagina is often shorter than the typical vagina.
11. Male hormones are present, but a receptor defect results in the body's inability to completely or partially process the male hormones.
12. Varies based on the degree of insensitivity to male hormones.
13. The individual will appear female at birth but may masculinize at puberty if left untreated.
14. The phenotype at puberty becomes male unless treated by exogenous hormones.
15. If the condition is undiagnosed, the child is raised as a female. At puberty, in some societies, the child becomes male or a third gender.
16. The genitals vary and may appear male at birth.
17. Excess male hormones are produced that lead to masculinization.
18. The phenotype will vary depending on the hormonal treatment.
19. Infants with severe masculinization may be raised as males.

# Notes

NOTES TO THE INTRODUCTION

1. Many people in the community want to abandon the term *intersex* in favor of the term *disorder of sex development* (DSD). I use both terms interchangeably throughout this book. This issue of appropriate terminology is discussed in more detail in chapter 8.

2. Melanie Blackless et al., "How Sexually Dimorphic Are We? Review and Synthesis," *American Journal of Human Biology* 151 (2000): 161. Some reports place the number of genital anomalies at birth as one in forty-five hundred. Peter A. Lee et al., "Consensus Statement on Management of Intersex Disorders," *Pediatrics* 118 (2006): e488–e500, http://pediatrics.aappublications.org/cgi/reprint/118/2/e488.

3. Some people combine the categories of gender presentation and gender role because they often overlap. I am using *gender presentation* to refer to a person's outward appearance including dress, hair style, use of makeup, and other markers that are typically associated with women or men. I am using *gender role* to refer to the position a person occupies in society that may have gender implications. Women are traditionally associated with caregiving roles, while men are typically presumed to be breadwinners.

4. Although most intersex conditions do not require medical intervention, some do require medical care. For example, congenital adrenal hyperplasia (CAH) may be life threatening and requires immediate medical treatment.

NOTES TO CHAPTER 1

1. Christopher J. Dewhurst and Ronald R. Gordon, *The Intersexual Disorders*, London: Balliere, Tindall and Cassell, 1969.

2. John Money, *Sex Errors of the Body and Related Syndromes: A Guide to Counseling Children, Adolescents, and Their Families*, Baltimore: Paul H. Brookes, 1994. Other experts would divide the factors slightly differently and include chromosomal sex, hypothalamic sex, fetal hormonal sex, pubertal hormonal sex, sex of assignment and rearing, internal morphological sex, external morphological sex, self-identified sex, and gonadal sex. Regardless of the specific categories used, medical experts all agree that sex determination is multifaceted and no one factor can be used to ascertain a person's sex.

3. "The Age of the Gonads" was a term developed by Alice Dreger. Alice Domurat Dreger, *Hermaphrodites and the Medical Invention of Sex*, Cambridge: Harvard University Press, 1998.

4. Ibid.

5. Alice Domurat Dreger, "A History of Intersexuality: From the Age of Gonads to the Age of Consent," *Journal of Clinical Ethics* 9 (1998): 345.

6. See, e.g., John Money, "Hermaphroditism: Recommendations Concerning Case Management," *Journal of Clinical Endocrinology and Metabolism* 4 (1956): 547; John Money, Joan G. Hampson, and John L. Hampson, "An Examination of Some Basic Sexual Concepts: The Evidence of Human Hermaphroditism," *Bulletin of the John Hopkins Hospital* 97 (1955): 301.

7. Suzanne J. Kessler, *Lessons from the Intersexed*, New Brunswick: Rutgers University Press, 1998.

8. An "acceptable" clitoris was one that was less than one centimeter in length. Phalluses between one and three centimeters were considered unacceptable and needed to be surgically altered. Anne Fausto-Sterling, *Sexing the Body: Gender Politics and the Construction of Sexuality*, New York: Basic Books, 2000.

9. Sherri G. Morris, "Twisted Lies: My Journey in an Imperfect Body," in *Surgically Shaping Children: Technology, Ethics, and the Pursuit of Normality*, ed. Erik Parens, Baltimore: Johns Hopkins University Press, 2006: 6–8.

10. See, e.g., Justine Schober and Pierre D. E. Mouriquand, "Long-Term Outcomes of Feminizing Genitoplasty for Intersex," in *Pediatric Surgery and Urology: Long-Term Outcomes*, ed. Mark D. Stringer, Keith T. Oldham, and Pierre D. E. Mouriquand, London: Saunders, 1998; Dreger, "History of Intersexuality," 345; Milton Diamond and H. Keith Sigmundson, "Sex Reassignment at Birth: Long-Term Review and Clinical Implications," *Archives of Pediatrics and Adolescent Medicine* 151 (1997): 298; William Reiner, "To Be Male or Female—That Is the Question," *Archives of Pediatrics and Adolescent Medicine* 151 (1997): 224; Fausto-Sterling, *Sexing the Body*; Kessler, *Lessons from the Intersexed*; Milton Diamond, "Pediatric Management of Ambiguous and Traumatized Genitalia," *Journal of Urology* 162 (1999): 1021; Kenneth I. Glassberg, "Gender Assignment and the Pediatric Urologist," *Journal of Urology* 161 (1999): 1308; Hazel Glenn Beh and Milton Diamond, "An Emerging Ethical and Medical Dilemma: Should Physicians Perform Sex Assignment Surgery on Infants with Ambiguous Genitalia?," *Michigan Journal of Gender and Law* 7 (2000): 1–63.

11. Diamond and Sigmundson, "Sex Reassignment at Birth," 298. For a more complete story of David Reimer's life, see John Colapinto, *As Nature Made Him: The Boy Who Was Raised as a Girl*, New York: HarperCollins, 2000.

12. See, e.g., Bernardo Ochoa, "Trauma of the External Genitalia in Children: Amputation of the Penis and Emasculation," *Journal of Urology* 160 (1998): 1116 (describing a study of seven children in Colombia that was conducted between 1960 and 1995); Susan J. Bradley et al., "Experiment of Nurture: Ablatio Penis at 2 Months, Sex Reassignment at 7 Months, and a Psychosexual Follow-Up in Young Adulthood," *Pediatrics* 102 (1998): 132–133 (reporting on a boy who was turned into a girl at seven months and who self-identifies as a bisexual female with recreational and occupational interests more typically identified with males).

13. William G. Reiner and John P. Gearhart, "Discordant Sexual Identity in Some Genetic Males with Cloacal Exstrophy Assigned to Female Sex at Birth," *New England Journal of Medicine* 350 (2004): 333–341.

14. Jiang-Ning Zhou et al., "A Sex Difference in the Human Brain and Its Relation to Transsexuality," *Nature* 378 (1995): 68–70; Frank Kruijver et al., "Male-to-Female Trans-

sexuals Have Female Neuron Numbers in the Central Subdivision of the Bed Nucleus of the Stria Terminals," *Journal of Clinical Endocrinology and Metabolism* 85 (2000): 2034–2041. A recent study indicates that white matter microstructure brain patterns for female-to-male transsexuals are more similar to subjects who share their gender identity than those who share their biological sex. Giuseppina Rametti et al., "White Matter Microstructure in Female to Male Transsexuals before Cross-Sex Hormonal Treatment: A Diffusion Tensor Imaging Study," *Journal of Psychiatric Research* 45 (2011): 199–204. Another study indicates that white matter microstructure brain patterns for male-to-female transsexuals is halfway between the patterns of males and females, indicating that complete masculinization during brain development did not occur for male-to-female transsexuals. Giuseppina Rametti et al., "The Microstructure of White Matter in Male to Female Transsexuals before Cross-Sex Hormonal Treatment: A DTI Study," *Journal of Psychiatric Research*, 2010, http://www.ncbi.nlm.nih.gov/pubmed/21195418.

15. Peter A. Lee et al., "Consensus Statement on Management of Intersex Disorders," *Pediatrics* 118 (2006): e488–e500, http://pediatrics.aappublications.org/cgi/reprint/118/2/e488.

16. Ibid., e491.

17. Anne Tamar-Mattis, executive director of Advocates for Informed Choice, personal interview, Aug. 30, 2010.

18. In some cases, leaving the testicles in the abdominal cavity will lead to an increased risk of cancer, although the level of risk varies greatly with the specific condition. In many cases, the risk is not significant before puberty. Therefore, the decision could be delayed until children reach puberty and are able to make the choice themselves. Although in some cases gonadectomy is necessary, in many cases the decision can be safely delayed.

19. American Academy of Pediatrics, Committee on Genetics and Section on Endocrinology and Urology, "Evaluation of the Newborn with Developmental Anomalies of the External Genitalia," *Pediatrics* 106 (2000): 138–142.

20. Julie A. Greenberg, "Legal Aspects of Gender Assignment," *Endocrinologist* 13 (2003): 277.

21. S. M. Creighton, C. L. Minto, and S. I. Steele, "Objective Cosmetic and Anatomical Outcomes at Adolescence of Feminizing Surgery for Ambiguous Genitalia Done in Childhood," *Lancet* 358 (2001): 124–125.

22. N. K. Alizai, F. M. Thomas, and R. J. Lilford, "Feminizing Genitoplasty for Congenital Adrenal Hyperplasia: What Happens at Puberty?," *Journal of Urology* 161 (1999): 1588–1591.

23. Joel Frader et al., "Health Care Professionals and Intersex Conditions," *Archives of Pediatrics and Adolescent Medicine* 158 (2004): 426–428.

24. Lee et al., "Consensus Statement on Management of Intersex Disorders," e491.

25. Katrina A Karkazis, "Early Genital Surgery to Remain Controversial," *Pediatrics* 118 (2006): 814–815.

26. Claudia Wiesemann et al., "Ethical Principles and Recommendations for the Medical Management of Differences of Sex Development (DSD)/Intersex in Children and Adolescents," *European Journal of Pediatrics* 169 (2010): 671–679, http://springerlink.com/content/875242220h6211vu/fulltext.pdf.

27. Melissa Parisi et al., "A Gender Assessment Team: Experience with 250 Patients over a Period of 25 Years," *Genetics in Medicine* 9 (2007): 348–357.

28. See, e.g., Saroj Nimkarn and Maria New, "Prenatal Diagnosis and Treatment of Congenital Adrenal Hyperplasia," *Hormone Research* 67 (2007): 53–60.

29. Catherine Elton, "A Prenatal Treatment Raises Questions of Medical Ethics," *Time*, June 18, 2010, http://www.time.com/time/health/article/0,8599,1996453,00.html.

30. Noel P. French et al., "Repeated Antenatal Corticosteroids: Effects on Cerebral Palsy and Childhood Behavior," *American Journal of Obstetrics and Gynecology* 190 (2004): 588–595.

31. See, e.g., Tata Hirvikoski et al., "Cognitive Functions in Children at Risk for Congenital Adrenal Hyperplasia Treated Prenatally with Dexamethasone," *Journal of Clinical Endocrinology and Metabolism* 92 (2007): 542–548.

32. Doctors have also implied that dexamethasone may also reduce the incidence of lesbianism and masculine behavior. Chapter 10 contains a more detailed discussion of this issue.

33. Jaime Frias et al., "American Academy of Pediatrics: Technical Report: Congenital Adrenal Hyperplasia," *Pediatrics* 106, no. 6 (2000): 1511–1518.

34. Lee et al., "Consensus Statement on Management of Intersex Disorders," e491.

35. Ibid.

36. Anne Tamar-Mattis, "Research into Outcomes of Treatment for Children with Differences of Sex Development Demands Caution, *Endocrine Today*, June 1, 2010, http://www.endocrinetoday.com/view.aspx?rid=65325.

37. Morris, "Twisted Lies," 8.

38. Jennifer Yang, Diane Felsen, and Dix P. Poppas, "Nerve Sparing Ventral Clitoroplasty: Analysis of Clitoral Sensitivity and Viability," *Journal of Urology* 178, no. 4 (2007): 1598–1601.

39. Alice Dreger and Ellen Feder, "Bad Vibrations," *Bioethics Forum* (blog), Hastings Center, June 16, 2010, http://www.thehastingscenter.org/Bioethicsforum/Post.aspx?id=4730&amp%3Bblogid=140&terms=dreger+and+%23filename+*.html.

40. Antonia Zerbisias, "Cornell Surgeon under Attack for Sex Testing on Girls," *Toronto Star*, June 23, 2010.

NOTES TO CHAPTER 2

1. Elizabeth Weil, "What If It's (Sort of) a Boy and (Sort of) a Girl?," *New York Times Magazine*, Sept. 24, 2006, http://www.nytimes.com/2006/09/24/magazine/24intersexkids.html?pagewanted=1&_r=2.

2. Although this book advocates greater oversight by an uninvolved person or entity, this proposal should not be interpreted as a criticism of parents who make the decision to have their child undergo genital cosmetic surgery or physicians who perform these procedures. Parents are in a very difficult situation and are making decisions out of love for their child and a desire to do what is in their child's best interests. Similarly, doctors are suggesting procedures that they believe will benefit their patients.

3. Alyssa Connell Lareau, "Who Decides? Gender Normalizing Surgery on Intersexed Infants," *Georgetown Law Journal* 92 (2000): 129; Hazel Glenn Beh and Milton Diamond, "An Emerging Ethical and Medical Dilemma: Should Physicians Perform Sex Assignment on Infants with Ambiguous Genitalia?," *Michigan Journal of Gender and Law* 7 (2000): 1; Bruce E. Wilson and William G. Reiner, "Management of Intersex: A Shifting Paradigm,"

*Journal of Clinical Ethics* 9 (1998): 360; Kenneth Kipnis and Milton Diamond, "Pediatric Ethics in the Surgical Assignment of Sex," *Journal of Clinical Ethics* 9 (1998): 398; Milton Diamond and Keith Sigmundson, "Management of Intersexuality: Guidelines for Dealing with Persons with Ambiguous Genitalia," *Archives of Pediatrics and Adolescent Medicine* 151 (1997): 1046; Cheryl Chase, "Surgical Progress Is Not the Answer to Intersexuality," *Journal Clinical Ethics* 9 (1998): 385; Cheryl Chase, "What Is the Agenda of the Intersex Patient Advocacy Movement?," *Endocrinologist* 13, no. 3 (2003): 240–242, available online at http://www.isna.org/agenda.

4. Erik Parens, "Introduction: Thinking about Surgically Shaping Children," in *Surgically Shaping Children: Technology, Ethics, and the Pursuit of Normality*, ed. Erik Parens, Baltimore: Johns Hopkins University Press, 2008: xxix.

5. Katrina Karkazis, *Fixing Sex: Intersex, Medical Authority, and Lived Experience*, Durham: Duke University Press, 2008: 134–135.

6. See, e.g., J. Daaboul and J. Frader, "Ethics and the Management of the Patient with Intersex: A Middle Way," *Journal of Pediatric Endocrinology and Metabolism* 14 (2001): 1575–1583; Robert M. Blizzard, "Intersex Issues: A Series of Continuing Conundrums," *Pediatrics* 110 (2002): 616–621, http://pediatrics.aappublications.org/cgi/content/full/110/3/616; British Association of Paediatric Surgeons Working Party on the Surgical Management of Children Born with Ambiguous Genitalia, "Statement of the British Association of Paediatric Surgeons Working Party on the Surgical Management of Children Born with Ambiguous Genitalia," July 2001 (on file with author); S. F. Ahmed, S. Morrison, and I. A. Hughes, "Intersex and Gender Assignment: The Third Way?," *Archives of Disease in Childhood* 89 (2004): 847; Claudia Wiesemann et al., "Ethical Principles and Recommendations for the Medical Management of Differences of Sex Development (DSD)/Intersex in Children and Adolescents," *European Journal of Pediatrics* 169 (2010): 671–679, http://springerlink.com/content/875242220h6211vu/fulltext.pdf.

7. Karkazis, *Fixing Sex*, 134–135; Melissa Parisi et al., "A Gender Assessment Team: Experience with 250 Patients over a Period of 25 Years," *Genetics in Medicine* 9 (2007): 348–357.

8. Posted in comments section of online version of Weil, "What If It's (Sort of) a Boy and (Sort of) a Girl?"

9. H. F. L. Meyer-Bahlburg et al., "Attitudes of Adult 46, XY Intersex Persons to Clinical Management Policies," *Journal of Urology* 171 (2004): 1615–1619.

10. South Africa considered adopting legislation but thus far has not done so. South African Press Association, "Legislation Mooted to Regulate Intersex Surgery," 2004 WL 99626478. The city of San Francisco has also held hearings on this issue and issued a report condemning current practices: Human Rights Commission of the City of San Francisco, "A Human Rights Investigation into the Medical 'Normalization' of Intersex People: A Report of a Hearing of the San Francisco Human Rights Commission," April 28, 2005, http://www.sf-hrc.org/ftp/uploadedfiles/sfhumanrights/Committee_Meetings/Lesbian_Gay_Bisexual_Transgender/SFHRC%20Intersex%20Report(1).pdf. For a thorough discussion of the findings of this commission, see chapter 10.

11. "Gender Warrior Wins Case against Surgeon," *Deutsche Welle*, June 2, 2008, http://www.dw-world.de/dw/article/0,2144,3111505,00.html.

12. This chapter focuses on practices in the United States. The rules regarding informed consent vary by jurisdiction, but the requirement of informed consent is a well accepted medical and legal doctrine in many countries.

13. American Academy of Pediatrics, Committee on Bioethics, "Informed Consent, Parental Permission, and Assent in Pediatric Practice," *Pediatrics* 95 (1995): 314.

14. See, e.g., Troxel v. Granville, 530 U.S. 57 660, 667 (2000) (involving a parent's right to determine visitation by grandparents); Parham v. J.R., 442 U.S. 584, 604 (1979) (involving parents' right to institutionalize their child with a psychiatric condition).

15. In addition to the cases discussed in this chapter, litigation regarding parental consent may occur when parents refuse to agree to a medically recommended procedure. These cases typically arise when a doctor suggests a potentially life-saving treatment for a child and the parents refuse to consent because the procedure violates the parents' religious beliefs. Those cases involve unique issues involving the First Amendment. Cases involving infants with an intersex condition are not analogous to the religious refusal cases for two reasons. First, the intersex cases involve doctors and parents who agree, as opposed to the religious refusal cases, in which the doctor is recommending a procedure and the parent is refusing. Second, the parental decision in the intersex cases is not based on religious practices and therefore does not involve First Amendment issues.

16. In the Matter of Romero, 790 P.2d 819 (Colo. 1990); Estate of C.W., 640 A.2d 427 (Pa. Super. 1994).

17. David R. Carson and Deborah A. Dorfman, "Investigative Report Regarding the 'Ashley Treatment,'" Washington Protection and Advocacy System, May 8, 2007, http://www.disabilityrightswa.org/home/Full_Report_InvestigativeReportRegardingtheAshley-Treatment.pdf.

18. Ibid. WPAS is now called Disability Rights Washington. For a more detailed report of this case, see the discussion of the Ashley case in chapter 10.

19. Buck v. Bell, 274 U.S. 200, 207 (1927).

20. Skinner v. Oklahoma, 316 U.S. 535 (1942). *Skinner* involved an Oklahoma statute that allowed the government to sterilize habitual criminals. A constitutional claim based on the fundamental right to reproductive freedom must be based on a governmental act and not based on the actions of private individuals. Therefore, a doctor (who is not employed by the state) or a parent could not be held liable for violating a child's constitutionally protected right to reproduction. Because reproduction is considered a fundamental right, however, a number of states have limited the ability of private actors to engage in actions that affect reproductive freedom.

21. States that have adopted legislation controlling the sterilization of people who are not competent to consent include Colorado (Colo. Rev. Stat. Ann. §§ 27-10.5-128–27-10.5-131 (West Supp. 1997)); Connecticut (Conn. Gen. Stat. Ann. §§ 45a-691–45a-700 (West 1997)); Maine (Me. Rev. Stat. Ann. tit. 34, §§ 7001–7016 (West 1998)); Ohio (Ohio Rev. Code. Ann. § 5123.86 (Anderson Supp. 1997)); Oregon (Ore. Rev. Stat. §§ 436.205–436.335 (1995)); and Vermont (Vt. Stat. Ann. tit. 18, §§ 8705–8716 (1987)). In states that do not have controlling legislation, courts have ruled that these procedures cannot be performed without a court order. See, e.g., In re Hayes, 608 P.2d 635 (Wa. 1980); In the Matter of Romero, 790 P.2d 819 (Colo. 1990); Estate of C.W., 640 A.2d 427 (Pa. Super. 1994).

22. Carson and Dorfman, "Investigative Report Regarding the 'Ashley Treatment.'"

23. Current technology does not exist that would allow CAIS women to reproduce. Presently, the gonads cannot produce sperm that could be used for reproduction. It is possible, however, that future technology could allow for reproductive ability. When doctors make their recommendations, the potential for reproduction should be considered.

24. In an unpublished opinion, a doctor was held liable for removing gonads and rendering a minor infertile when he proceeded without the consent of the minor or her parents. See, e.g., Before the Minnesota Board of Medical Practice Stipulation and Order in the Matter of the Medical License of Michael H. Wipf, M.D., Date of Birth 1/31/1953, License Number 28,237 (on file with author).

25. Doctors were responsible for initiating the case in Colombia that eventually resulted in the Constitutional Court of Colombia imposing safeguards to protect infants born with an intersex condition. Doctors were concerned that they might be held liable for performing cosmetic genital surgery, so they told the parents that they would not proceed without a court order.

26. No oversight is typically imposed as long as the procedure is solely to benefit the patient. If the procedure is being performed to benefit another person—for example, removing a kidney for transplant into the patient's sibling—court approval is necessary.

27. Carson and Dorfman, "Investigative Report Regarding the 'Ashley Treatment,'" 18–19.

28. Ibid.

29. Law professor Alicia Ouellette has argued that parental decisions authorizing medical and surgical interventions to sculpt children's bodies should be analyzed under a trust-based construct that would require neutral third-party approval, rather than giving complete deference to the parents' decisions. Alicia Ouelette, "Shaping Parental Authority over Children's Bodies," *Indiana Law Journal* 85 (2010): 955.

30. Sentencia No. SU-337/99; Sentencia No. T-551/99. These decisions are reported in Spanish and can be found at http://www.isna.org/node/21. A translation of a portion of decision SU-337/99 into English appears in "The Rights of Intersexed Infants and Children: Decision of the Colombian Constitutional Court, Bogotá, Colombia, 12 May 1999 (SU-337/99)," trans. Nohemy Solórzano-Thompson, in *Transgender Rights*, ed. Paisley Currah, Richard M. Juang, and Shannon Price Minter, Minneapolis: University of Minnesota Press, 2006: 122–138.

31. Ibid., 130.

32. Ibid.

33. Ibid.

34. Lareau, "Who Decides?"; Beh and Diamond, "An Emerging Ethical and Medical Dilemma"; Wilson and Reiner, "Management of Intersex"; Kipnis and Diamond, "Pediatric Ethics in the Surgical Assignment of Sex"; Diamond and Sigmundson, "Management of Intersexuality"; Chase, "Surgical Progress Is Not the Answer to Intersexuality"; Chase, "What Is the Agenda of the Intersex Patient Advocacy Movement?"

35. Laws do not typically provide a precise age for minors to consent to medical procedures. The determination is based on the procedure involved and the ability of the adolescent to assess the risks and benefits. In the one decision specifically addressing this issue for minors with an intersex condition, the Constitutional Court of Colombia stated that there is no clear age and that the capacity to assent depends on the minor's ability to assess and understand the risks and benefits of the decision. "The Rights of Intersexed Infants and Children," 135.

36. Committee on Bioethics, "Informed Consent, Parental Permission, and Assent in Pediatric Practice," *Pediatrics* 95 (1995): 314–317.

37. Christine Muckle, "Giving a Voice to Intersex Individuals through Hospital Ethics Committees," *Wisconsin Law Review* (2006): 987; Julie A. Greenberg, "International Legal Developments Protecting the Autonomy Rights of Sexual Minorities: Who Should Decide the Appropriate Treatment for an Intersex Child?," in *Ethics and Intersex*, ed. Sharon E. Sytsma, Dordrecht, the Netherlands: Springer, 2006: 97–99.

38. When the Ashley treatment (discussed in more detail in chapter 10) became a matter of public debate, a group of disability experts and advocates convened a group to address these complex issues. Their published report provides an excellent discussion of the advantages and disadvantages of different alternatives when the issue involves the administration of growth attenuation treatment of a profoundly disabled child. Benjamin S. Wilfond et al., "Navigating Growth Attenuation in Children with Profound Disabilities: Children's Interests, Family Decision-Making and Community Concerns," *Hastings Center Report*, Nov.–Dec. 2010: 27.

39. Anne Tamar-Mattis, "Exceptions to the Rule: Curing the Law's Failure to Protect Intersex Infants," *Berkeley Journal of Gender and the Law* 21 (2006): 89.

40. Suzanne J. Kessler, *Lessons from the Intersexed*, New Brunswick: Rutgers University Press, 1998: 101.

41. Ibid., 102–103.

42. Jennifer E. Dayner, Peter A. Lee, and Christopher P. Houk, "Medical Treatment of Intersex: Parental Perspectives," *Journal of Urology* 172 (2004): 1764.

43. See, e.g., website of Aventura Center for Cosmetic Surgery and Hair Restoration, http://www.aventuracosmeticsurgery.com/index.cfm/PageID/5395, offering "designer vaginas" and labia sculpting.

44. Lih Mei Liao and Sarah M. Creighton, "Requests for Cosmetic Genitoplasty: How Should Healthcare Providers Respond?," *British Medical Journal* 334 (2007): 1090–1092, http://bmj.com/cgi/content/full/334/7603/1090.

45. In re A, 16 FLR 715 (Family Court of Australia 1993).

46. Ibid.

47. Thamar Klein, "Intersex and Transgender Activism in South Africa," *Liminalis* 3 (2009): 15.

48. See, e.g., Robin Fretwell Wilson, "Hospital Ethics Committees as the Forum of Last Resort: An Idea Whose Time Has Not Come," *North Carolina Law Review* 76 (1998): 353. Fretwell recommends that courts be the ultimate decision maker in end-of-life cases.

49. Tamar-Mattis, "Exceptions to the Rule," 97–98.

50. When a group of disability experts, parents, and advocates convened to examine a similar decision regarding growth attenuation treatment of profoundly disabled children, they acknowledged that consensus building was impossible and instead reached a middle ground compromise position. They recommended that parents be allowed to continue to make this decision, just as they make other medical decisions for their minor children. They also recommended that doctors and hospitals that perform these procedures institute special safeguards and employ a thorough decision making process including the involvement of an ethics committee or consultant. Wilfond et al., "Navigating Growth Attenuation in Children with Profound Disabilities," 27. The report included dissenting opinions from some participants. Norman Fost believed that third parties do not have an adequate interest in the outcome and that public opinion should not be considered in the decision making process. Eva Feder Kittay argued that these procedures constitute

discrimination against the profoundly impaired because they would not be allowed on an unimpaired child. Sue Swenson and Sandy Walker presented two opposing parental perspectives about these procedures. Swenson argued that procedures that do not fix an underlying disorder should not be allowed and Walker asserted that parents should be accorded greater deference.

## NOTES TO CHAPTER 3

1. Anne Fausto-Sterling, "Two Sexes Are Not Enough," *Nova Online*, PBS. org, http://www.pbs.org/cgi-bin/wgbh/printable.pl?http%3A%2F%2Fwww.pbs. org%2Fwgbh%2Fnova%2Fgender%2Ffs.html.

2. Sex classification systems are also important outside of law and medicine. Other authoritative bodies have established rules for determining a person's sex that may be at variance with legal and medical rules. For example, people with an intersex condition competing in world class athletic events may be subjected to lengthy procedures involving gynecologists, endocrinologists, psychologists, and hematologists before they are allowed to participate in women's athletic events. In 2006, the International Association of Athletics Federation stripped an Indian runner—who had been identified at birth as a girl, had been raised as a female, and self-identified as a woman—of her silver medal, when it determined that she had a Y chromosome. In 2009, Caster Semenya, a South African runner, won the gold medal in the women's 800 meter race at the 2009 World Championships. Her right to compete as a woman was challenged. Although she was allowed to retain her gold medal, she was the subject of international headlines and articles debating her "true" sex.

3. This part of the book focuses on the determination of a person's "legal" sex. People with an intersex condition may also suffer discriminatory treatment unrelated to the determination of the person's legal sex status. For example, transsexuals have been denied Medicare or insurance coverage for their treatment. People with an intersex condition may also be subjected to other discriminatory treatment that has been directed against transsexuals. The legal framework for analyzing these issues is discussed in chapter 10.

## NOTES TO CHAPTER 4

1. The facts are as reported in *In Marriage of C and D (falsely called C)*, 35 FLR 340 (1979). The only embellishment that I have added to the description of this case is to give the parties fictional names, rather than referring to them as C and D as the court did.

2. The following facts are reported in *W v. W*, 58 BMLR 15 (Fam. 111 2001). The only change that I have made to the description of the case is to give the parties fictional names, rather than referring to them as W and W.

3. *W v. W*, 58 BMLR 15 (Fam. 111 2001).

4. The marriage cases discussed in this chapter do not involve cases of fraud. In other words, the person challenging the marriage has not alleged that the marriage should be declared invalid because the intersex or transsexual spouses misled their mates about their condition. Instead, litigants are using the state's heterosexual marriage laws for monetary purposes or to gain an advantage in a custody dispute. Cases have been brought by (1) spouses who wanted to avoid paying spousal support, (2) an estranged stepchild who

wanted to be the sole beneficiary of his father's multimillion dollar estate, (3) a doctor who wanted to avoid having to pay damages to a transsexual wife when his malpractice caused her husband's death, and (4) spouses who wanted to deny their former mates the ability to coparent.

5. Same-sex marriages are banned in most jurisdictions. Countries recognizing same-sex marriages include Argentina, Belgium, Canada, the Netherlands, Norway, Portugal, South Africa, Spain, and Sweden. Six jurisdictions in the United States allow same-sex couples to wed: Connecticut, the District of Columbia, Iowa, Massachusetts, New Hampshire, and Vermont. In addition, some municipalities—for example, Mexico City—recognize same-sex marriages.

6. Mary Coombs, "Sexual Dis-Orientation: Transgendered People and Same-Sex Marriage," *UCLA Women's Law Journal* 8 (1998): 219.

7. See, e.g., In re Marriage Cases, 43 Cal. 4th 757, 825–828, 183 P.3d 384, 431 (2008); Perry v. Schwarzenegger, 704 F. Supp. 2d 921 (N.D. Cal. 2010).

8. Ellen C. Perrin and the Committee on Psychosocial Aspects of Child and Family Health, "Technical Report: Co-parent or Second-Parent Adoption by Same-Sex Parents," *Pediatrics* 109 (2002): 342–343. No scientific evidence supports a finding that parenting effectiveness or the psychological well-being of children is related to parental sexual orientation. Proceedings of the American Psychological Association, "Sexual Orientation, Parents, & Children," adopted July 28 and 30, 2004, http://www.apa.org/about/governance/council/policy/parenting.aspx; Rachel H. Farr, Stephen L. Forssell , "Parenting and Child Development in Adoptive Families: Does Parental Sexual Orientation Matter?," *Applied Developmental Science* 14, no. 3 (2010): 164–178; Nanette Gartrell and Henny Bos, "US National Longitudinal Lesbian Family Study: Psychological Adjustment of 17-Year-Old Adolescents," *Pediatrics* 126, no. 1 (2010): 1–9.

9. Gender Recognition Act 2004: Chapter 7, London: Office of Public Sector Information, 2004, http://www.opsi.gov.uk/acts/acts2004/ukpga_20040007_en_1.

10. W v. W, 58 BMLR 15 (Fam. 111 2001).

11. Corbett v. Corbett, 2 All E.R. 33 (1970).

12. In *Anonymous v. Anonymous*, 325 N.Y.S.2d 499 (NY Sup. Ct. 1971), the court invalidated a marriage between a male and a male-to-female transsexual. It did not state which factors should be used to determine sex but opined that "mere removal of the male organs would not, in and of itself, change a person into a true female" (ibid., 500). Three years later, in *B v. B*, 355 N.Y.S.2d 712 (N.Y. Sup. Ct. 1974), the court invalidated a marriage between a woman and a postoperative female-to-male transsexual. Once again, the court did not determine which factors should be used to determine sex. It held that physical incapacity for sexual relations is grounds for an annulment and that the transsexual husband did not have the "necessary apparatus to enable defendant to function as a man for the purposes of procreation" (ibid., 717).

13. In *In re Ladrach*, 513 N.E.2d 828 (Ohio 1987), the court held that a postoperative male-to-female transsexual still retained male chromosomes and therefore could not marry in the female role because she was still legally a male.

14. In *C v. C*, 1992 Ont. C.J. Lexis 1518 (1992), a female-to-male transsexual, who had received hormone treatments, had undergone a hysterectomy, and had her breasts surgically removed, married a woman. The court annulled the marriage and held that he could not qualify as a legal male because the external genitalia still appeared female.

In *M v. M*, 42 RFL (2d) 55 (1984), the court was faced with determining the validity of a marriage between a male and a nonoperative female-to-male transsexual who had all female attributes except for a male gender self-identity. Ironically, the court held that the marriage was invalid because the transsexual spouse could not legally marry a man because "she" had a "latent" inability to engage in heterosexual intercourse with a man. The court reasoned as follows: "If my understanding of the transsexual personality is correct, although the physical capacity for normal heterosexual intercourse may exist, there also exist psychological factors, inherent in the personality, which preclude or otherwise inhibit the actual exercise of such physical capacity. These psychological factors may be initially patent, in which case there is simply no capacity to exercise the function, or they may be latent or suppressed, in which case the capacity to exercise the function does exist, and may indeed be exercised, but the exercise thereof simply makes patent what was earlier latent and the act of heterosexual intercourse thereby becomes abhorrent to the point where it becomes, in effect, a continuing incapacity. The incapacitating condition was present in the marriage from its outset; it was merely triggered into transition from the state of latent potentiality into the state of patent actuality by the circumstance of the intimacy arising out of the married relationship, which, being heterosexual in nature, was incompatible with the inherent nature of the respondent. I find, therefore, that there existed at the outset of this marriage a latent physical incapacity for natural heterosexual intercourse, which incapacity became patent only subsequent to the solemnization of the marriage, of such consequence as would render the said marriage voidable." Ibid.

15. Lim Ying v. Hiok Kian Ming Eric, SLR Lexis 184 (1991).

16. In *W v. W*, 2 SALR 308 (1976), a South African court voided a marriage between a male and a postoperative male-to-female transsexual. Even though the marriage had been consummated, the court held that the wife had only "artificial attributes" of a woman and was therefore only a "pseudo-woman" who could not marry a man.

17. Rees v. United Kingdom, 2 FLR 111, 9 EHRR 57 (Eur. Ct. of H.R. 1986); Cossey v. United Kingdom, 2 FLR 492, 13 EHRR 622 (Eur. Ct. of H.R. 1991); Sheffield and Horsham v. United Kingdom, 27 EHRR 163 (Eur. Ct. of H.R. 1998).

18. M.T. v. J.T., 355 A.2d 204 (N.J. Super. A.D. 1976)

19. Ibid. According to this court, because sexual capacity is necessary for consummation of a marriage, the genitalia must be capable of sexual intercourse.

20. Attorney General v. Otahuhu Family Court, 1 NZLR 603 (1991).

21. Ibid.

22. Case of I. v. the United Kingdom, 36 EHRR 53 (Eur. Ct of H.R. 2002); Goodwin v. United Kingdom, 35 EHRR 18 (Eur. Ct. of H.R. 2002).

23. See, e.g., Rees v. United Kingdom, App. No. 9532/81, 9 Eur. H.R. Rep. 56 (1987); Cossey v. United Kingdom, App. No. 10843/84, 13 Eur. H.R. Rep. 622 (1990).

24. Case of I. v. the United Kingdom, 36 EHRR 53 (Eur. Ct of H.R. 2002); Goodwin v. United Kingdom, 35 EHRR 18 (Eur. Ct. of H.R. 2002).

25. Gender Recognition Act 2004: Chapter 7, London: Office of Public Sector Information, 2004, http://www.opsi.gov.uk/acts/acts2004/ukpga_20040007_en_1.

26. Attorney General v. Kevin, 172 FLR 300, 348 (2003).

27. Vecchione v. Vecchione, Civ. No 96D003769, reported in *L.A. Daily Journal*, Nov. 26, 1997: 1. This decision is an unpublished opinion.

28. Carter v. Carter (decision on file with author). The Louisiana decision was not published.

29. The 800 page trial court opinion can be found at www.transgenderlaw.org/Kantarasjulydecision.pdf.

30. In re Estate of Gardiner, 22 P.3d 1086 (Kan. Ct. App. 2001), rev'd 42 P.3d 120 (Kan. 2002).

31. In re Lovo-Lara, 23 I. & N. Dec. 746 (B.I.A. 2005); In re Ady Oren, 2004 WL 1167318 (B.I.A. 2004); In re Widener, 2004 WL 2375065 (B.I.A. 2004). Generally, in immigration cases, a marriage involving a transsexual spouse will be considered a valid heterosexual marriage if it would be valid in the state where the applicants reside.

32. In re Estate of Gardiner, 42 P.3d 120 (Kan. 2002).

33. Kantaras v. Kantaras, 884 So. 2d 155 (Fla. Dist. Ct. App. 2004).

34. Littleton v. Prange, 9 S.W.3d 223 (Tex. App. 1999).

35. In re Nash, 2003 WL 23097095 (Ohio Ct. App. 2003).

36. In re Estate of Gardiner, 22 P.3d 1086, 1110 (Kan. Ct. App. 2001), rev'd 42 P.3d 120 (Kan. 2002).

37. In re Nash, 2003 WL 23097095, at *6 (Ohio Ct. App. 2003).

38. In re Estate of Gardiner, 42 P.3d 120, 135 (Kan. 2002).

39. Kantaras v. Kantaras, 884 So. 2d 155, 159 (Fla. Dist. Ct. App. 2004).

40. In re Estate of Gardiner, 42 P.3d 120, 213 (Kan. 2002).

41. National Women's Health Information Center, U.S. Department of Health and Human Services, "Infertility: Frequently Asked Questions," last updated July 1, 2009, http://www.womenshealth.gov/faq/infertility.cfm#b.

42. Littleton v. Prange, 9 S.W.3d 223, 231 (Tex. App. 1999).

43. See, e.g., Littleton v. Prange, 9 S.W.3d 223, 229 (Tex. App. 1999); In re Estate of Gardiner, 42 P.3d 120, 136 (Kan. 2002); Kantaras v. Kantaras, 884 So. 2d 155, 159 (Fla. Dist. Ct. App. 2004); In re Nash, 2003 WL 23097095, at 6 (Ohio Ct. App. 2003).

44. In re Marriage of Simmons, 825 N.E.2d 303, 309–310 (Ill. App. Ct. 2005).

45. See Jilly Beattie and Sara Lain, "The Wedding with Two Brides . . . and One Is a Man! Lesbian Lovers Both Wear a Dress for Britain's Weirdest-Ever Marriage; 'I Was a Chick-with-a-Dick, I Had My Op and Woke Up as a Girl'; Lesbians to Legally Marry Because One Is an Ex-Man," *People*, June 11, 1995: 2; "Oregon Couple Adds Twist to Love Story: The Bride and Groom Plan to Wed Legally, but Then the Man Intends to Have His Gender Altered," *Morning News Tribune* (Tacoma, Wash.), Dec. 14, 1996: A3; Michael Vigh, "Transsexual Weds Woman in Legally Recognized Union," *Salt Lake Tribune*, Feb. 5, 1999: C1.

46. Chuck Lindell, "In Marriage Cases, How Should Sex Be Determined?," *American Statesman*, May 6, 2010, http://www.statesman.com/news/local/in-marriage-cases-how-should-sex-be-determined-673181.html?cxntlid=cmg_cntnt_rss; Daniel Borunda, "One Partner's Male Birth Status Allows Two Women to Get Married," *Farmington (NM) Daily Times*, May 5, 2010, http://www.daily-times.com/ci_15020782.

47. Heather Cassell, "California Looms as Marriage Equality Battleground," *Bay Area Reporter*, July 5, 2007, http://www.ebar.com/news/article.php?sec=news&article=1972.


NOTES TO CHAPTER 5

1. In re McIntyre, 1996 WL 942100 (Pa. Com. Pl. 1996).

2. Gender Recognition Act 2004: Chapter 7, London: Office of Public Sector Information, 2004, http://www.opsi.gov.uk/acts/acts2004/ukpga_20040007_en_1.

3. Julie Butler, "X Marks the Spot for Intersex Alex," *West Australian*, Jan. 11, 2003.

4. Harmeet Shah Singh, "India's Third Gender Gets Own Identity in Voter Rolls," CNN.com, Nov. 12, 2009, http://edition.cnn.com/2009/WORLD/asiapcf/11/12/india.gender.voting/index.html.

5. Antonia Hoyler and Melissa Stewart, "Exclusive: Girl Who Made Legal History Celebrates 18th," *Daily Mirror* (London), May 17, 2006, http://www.mirror.co.uk/news/top-stories/2006/05/17/exclusive-girl-who-made-legal-history-celebrates-18th-115875-17090233/.

6. Anne Tamar-Mattis, executive director of Advocates for Informed Choice, personal interview, Aug. 30, 2010.

7. See Ala. Code § 22-9A-19(d) (2004); Ariz. Rev. Stat. Ann. § 36-337(a)(3) (2006); Ark. Code Ann. § 20-18-307(d) (2005); Cal. Health & Safety Code § 103425 (2006); Colo. Rev. Stat. § 25-2-115(4) (2006); Conn. Gen Stat. § 19a-42 (2004); Del. Code Ann. Tit. 16 § 3131(a) (2006); D.C. Code Ann. § 7-217(d) (2006); Fla. Stat. Ann. § 382.016 (2006), Administrative Code: Fla. Admin. Code Ann. r. 64V-1.003(1)(f) (2006); Ga. Code Ann. § 31-10-23(e) (2005); Haw. Rev. Stat. § 338-17.7(a)(4)(B) (2005); 410 Ill. Comp. Stat. Ann. § 535-17(1)(d) (2006); Iowa Code Ann. § 144.23(3) (2004); Admin. Code K.A.R. § 28-17-20(b)(1)(A)(i) (2006); Ky. Rev. Stat. Ann. § 213.121 (5) (2005); La. Rev. Stat. Ann. § 40:62 (2006); Me. Rev. Stat. Ann. Tit. 22, § 2705 (2005); Md. Code Ann., Health-General § 4-214 (b)(5) (2006); Mass. Gen. Laws Ann. Ch. 46 § 13(e) (2206); Mich. Comp. Laws § 333.2831(c) (2006); Mo. Ann. Stat. § 193.215(9) (2006); Mont. Code Ann. § 50-15-204 (2005), Admin. R. Mont. 37.8.106(6) (2005); Neb. Rev. Stat. § 71-604.01 (2005); Nev. Admin. Code. Ch. 440, § 130 (2006); N.H. Code Admin. R. He-P 7007.03(e) (2004); N.J. Stat. Ann. 26:8-40.12 (2006); N.M. Stat. Ann. § 24-14-25 (D) (2006); N.Y. Comp. Codes R. & Regs. Tit. 10, § 35.2 (2005), 24 RCNY Hlth. Code § 207.05(a)(5) (2005); N.C. Gen. Stat. §§ 130A-118(b)(4), (e) (2005); N.D. Cent. Code § 23-02.1-25 (2005), N.D. Admin. Code § 33-04-12-02 (2006); Or. Rev Stat. § 432.235(4) (2005); 35 Penn. Stat. § 450.603 (2005); R.I. Gen. Laws § 23-3-21, R.I. Code R. 14 170 001 §§ 35–37 (2004); Utah Code Ann. § 26-2-11 (2004); Va. Code Ann. § 32.1-269(E) (2006); Wis. Stat. Ann § 69.15 (2006); Wyo. Stat. Ann. § 35-1-424 (2005).

8. Dean Spade, "Documenting Gender," *Hastings Law Journal* 59 (2008): 832–841.

9. See Alaska Stat. § 18.50.290 (2005); Idaho Code § 39-250 (2005); Ind. Code Ann. § 16-37-2-10(b) (2006); Me. Rev. Stat. Ann. Tit. 22, § 2705 (2005); Minn. Stat. Ann. § 144.218 (2006); Miss. Code Ann. § 41-57-21 (2006); Ohio Rev. Code § 3705.15 (2006); 63 Okl. Stat. Ann. § 1-321 (2006), Okla. Admin. Code 310:105-3-3 (2006); S.C. Code Ann. § 44-63-150 (2005), S.C. Code Ann. Regs. 61-19 (2006); S.D. Admin. R. 44:09:05:02 (2006); Tex. Health & Safety Code Ann. § 192.011 (2006); 18 Vt. Stat. §§ 5075, 5076 (2005); W.Va. Code § 16-5-24 (2006), W.Va. Code St. R. § 64-32-6 (2006). Washington has not adopted a statute or administrative rule regarding birth certificate amendments, but the Department of Health's policy is to allow an amendment to the sex designation on the birth record. Dean Spade, "Documenting Gender," *Hastings Law Journal* 59 (2008): 840.

10. Alaska, Indiana, Maine, Minnesota, Mississippi, Oklahoma, South Carolina, South Dakota, Vermont, Washington, and West Virginia.

11. Spade, "Documenting Gender," 834.

12. In re Ladrach, 32 Ohio Misc. 2d 6, 513 N.E.2d 828 (Ohio Prob. Ct. 1987).

13. Spade, "Documenting Gender," 839–840.

14. Tenn. Code Ann. § 68-3-203(d) (2006).

15. Social Security Online, "RM 00203.215 Changing Numident Data—Other Than Name Change. B. Procedure—Evidence Required to Correct or Change Numident Data," https://secure.ssa.gov/poms.nsf/lnx/0110212200.

16. National Center for Transgender Equality, "Federal Documents: Changing Your Documentation," http://transequality.org/Issues/federal_documents.html#ss_gender.

17. U.S. Department of State, "7 Fam 1350 Appendix M: Gender Change," *Foreign Affairs Manual*, vol. 7, www.state.gov/documents/organization/143160.pdf.

18. Ibid. These new rules are a vast improvement over the rules the State Department first published in 2010. The original amended rules indicated that the drafters did not fully understand intersexuality and the difference between intersexuality and transsexuality. First, they titled the applicable section "Cases of Unspecified Gender," but the rules related to someone whose gender was improperly specified at birth rather than someone whose gender was not specified. In addition, the rules defined intersexuality as a discrepancy between the internal and external genitals. Not all intersex people have a discrepancy between their internal reproductive organs and their external genitalia and the term "internal genitals" does not accurately reflect the proper terminology for the internal reproductive system. Most important, the rules required that the intersex applicant undergo gender transition, which does not make sense for a number of reasons. After the State Department published these rules, intersex and transgender advocates requested amendments and the State Department complied.

19. Spade, "Documenting Gender," 822–829.

20. Hartin v. Dir. of the Bureau of Records, 347 N.Y.S.2d 515, 518 (N.Y. Sup. Ct. 1973).

21. In re Ladrach, 513 N.E.2d 828, 832 (Ohio Prob. 1987).

22. Hartin v. Dir. of the Bureau of Records, 347 N.Y.S.2d 515, 518 (N.Y. Sup. Ct. 1973).

23. K v. Health Division, Dept. of Human Resources, 277 Or. 371, 375–376 (Or. 1977).

24. This statement should not be interpreted as support for legislatures to adopt such statutes. If, however, that is the legislative concern, the issue should be addressed directly.

25. See Jilly Beattie and Sara Lain, "The Wedding with Two Brides . . . and One Is a Man! Lesbian Lovers Both Wear a Dress for Britain's Weirdest-Ever Marriage; 'I Was a Chick-with-a-Dick, I Had My Op and Woke Up as a Girl'; Lesbians to Legally Marry Because One Is an Ex-Man," *People*, June 11, 1995: 2; "Oregon Couple Adds Twist to Love Story: The Bride and Groom Plan to Wed Legally, but Then the Man Intends to Have His Gender Altered," *Morning News Tribune* (Tacoma, Wash.), Dec. 14, 1996: A3; Michael Vigh, "Transsexual Weds Woman in Legally Recognized Union," *Salt Lake Tribune*, Feb. 5, 1999: C1.

26. Disease and illness are not natural phenomena free from social construction. See, e.g., Dominic Murphy, "Concepts of Disease and Health," in *Stanford Encyclopedia of Philosophy*, http://plato.stanford.edu/entries/health-disease/.

NOTES TO CHAPTER 6

1. Patricia J. Williams, *The Alchemy of Race and Rights*, Cambridge: Harvard University Press, 1991: 123.

2. Tates v. Blanas, 2003 WL 23864868 (E.D. Cal. 2003).

3. See, e.g., Pitzer College's housing request form: "Gender-neutral housing provides a living environment where student housing is not restricted to traditional limitations imposed by gender and/or sex definitions. This option is ideal for students whose gender expression, gender identity and/or biological sex varies from the standard paradigm and for students who believe that their gender and/or biological sex should not be limiting factors in roommate decisions. Pitzer students are not restricted to selecting a roommate based on biological sex." http://www.pitzer.edu/student_life/residential_life/room_draw/Room_Draw_Preference_Form-Writable.pdf.

4. In re Estate of Gardiner, 42 P.3d 120 (Kan. 2002).

5. "Transgender MP in Toilet Fracas," *BBC News*, Oct. 28, 2006, http://news.bbc.co.uk/2/hi/6094782.stm.

6. See Ann Arbor, Mich., City Code, Chapter 112, § 9:160 (2009), available at http://www.municode.com/resources/gateway.asp?pid=11782&sid=22; City of Kalamazoo, Mich. Ordinance No. 1850, § 18-25 L (2009), http://www.kalamazoocity.org/docs/1850.pdf.

7. Goins v. West Group, 635 N.W.2d 717 (Minn. 2001).

8. Jennifer Levi and Daniel Redman, "The Cross-Dressing Case for Bathroom Equality," *Seattle University Law Review* 34 (2010): 143–144.

9. Goins v. West Group, 635 N.W.2d 717 (Minn. 2001).

10. Ibid., 722.

11. Ibid.

12. Hispanic Aids Forum v. Bruno, 792 N.Y.S.2d 43 (N.Y. App. Div. 2005).

13. Ibid., 47.

14. Cruzan v. Special School District #1, 294 F.3d 981 (Minn. 2002).

15. Seantain Cook, quoted in ACLU National Prison Project, Stop Prisoner Rape, "Still in Danger: The Ongoing Threat of Sexual Violence against Transgender Prisoners," 4, http://www.spr.org/pdf/stillindanger.pdf.

16. Darren Rosenblum, "Trapped in Sing Sing: Transgendered Prisoners Caught in the Gender Binarism," *Michigan Journal of Gender and Law* 6 (1999): 522; Sydney Tarzwell, "The Gender Lines Are Marked with Razor Wire: Addressing State Prison Policies and Practices for the Management of Transgender Prisoners," *Columbia Human Rights Law Review* 38 (2006): 190–196.

17. DiMarco v. Wyoming Dep't of Corrections, 2007 WL 172189 (Wyo. 2007). The only other reported case involving the housing of a prisoner with an intersex condition involved Yasmin Tucker, a woman with congenital adrenal hyperplasia (CAH). Tucker alleged that her Eighth Amendment rights were violated when she was housed in the alternative lifestyle ward with transgender and gay prisoners rather than with the female population and when she was strip-searched by male prison guards. The court ruled that the prison's decisions did not violate the Eighth Amendment because Tucker was not exposed to a substantial risk of serious harm and the prison officials did not act with deliberate indifference to a known risk to Tucker. The court found that Tucker admitted that she did not appear to be female and that the prison did not understand her condition, and under these circumstances, it was not unreasonable for the prison to house her in a separate cell on the special unit. Tucker v. Evans, 2009 WL 799175 (E.D. Mich. 2009).

18. Quoted in ACLU National Prison Project, Stop Prisoner Rape, "Still in Danger," 7.

19. Farmer v. Brennan, 511 U.S. 825 (1994).

20. Prison Litigation Reform Act, 42 U.S.C. § 1997e (2000).

21. Lamb v. Maschner, 633 F. Supp. 351 (D. Kan. 1986).

22. Farmer v. Carlson, 685 F. Supp. 1335 (M.D. Pa. 1988).

23. Terry Kogan, "Sex-Separation in Public Restrooms: Law, Architecture, and Gender," *Michigan Journal of Gender and Law* 14 (2007): 1.

24. Ibid., 57.


NOTES TO CHAPTER 7

1. Katrina Karkazis, *Fixing Sex: Intersex, Medical Authority, and Lived Experience*, Durham: Duke University Press, 2008.

2. Ibid., 134–135.


NOTES TO CHAPTER 8

1. When I refer to Bo Laurent's publications, I use the name that she used for the publication.

2. Intersex Society of North America, "Welcome," *Hermaphrodites with Attitude* 1 (Winter 1994), http://www.isna.org/files/hwa/winter1995.pdf. The effort to remove the stigma from the term *hermaphrodite* has not been successful. Most people with an intersex condition believe the term sensationalizes their bodies and dehumanizes them. Therefore, the intersex movement now advocates that the term not be used.

3. Katrina Karkazis, *Fixing Sex: Intersex, Medical Authority, and Lived Experience*, Durham: Duke University Press, 2008: 254.

4. Eli Nevada and Cheryl Chase, Intersex Society of North America, "Natural Allies," *Hermaphrodites with Attitude* 2 (Summer 1995): 1, 11, http://www.isna.org/files/hwa/summer1995.pdf.

5. Karkazis, *Fixing Sex*, 238.

6. Nancy Ehrenreich with Mark Barr, "Intersex Surgery, Female Genital Cutting, and the Selective Condemnation of 'Cultural Practices,'" *Harvard Civil Rights–Civil Liberties Law Review* 40 (2005): 76. For further detail about this rift, see chapter 9.

7. Federal Prohibition of Female Genital Mutilation Act of 1995, Pub. L. No. 104-208, 100 Stat. 3009 (1996); 18 U.S.C. § 116 (1996).

8. Although David Reimer was not born with an intersex condition, when he lost his penis in a botched circumcision, he was treated under the same protocol applied to infants with an intersex condition.

9. Suzanne J. Kessler, "The Medical Construction of Gender: Case Management of Intersexual Infants," *Signs: Journal of Women in Culture and Society* 16 (1990): 3–26.

10. Suzanne J. Kessler, *Lessons from the Intersexed*, New Brunswick: Rutgers University Press, 1998.

11. Anne Fausto-Sterling, "The Five Sexes: Why Male and Female Are Not Enough," *Sciences* 33 (1993): 20–25.

12. Anne Fausto-Sterling, *Sexing the Body: Gender Politics and the Construction of Sexuality*, New York: Basic Books, 2000.

13. Alice Domurat Dreger, *Hermaphrodites and the Medical Invention of Sex*, Cambridge: Harvard University Press, 1998.

14. Julie A. Greenberg, "Defining Male and Female: Intersexuality and the Collision between Law and Biology" *Arizona Law Review* 41 (1999): 265; Hazel Glenn Beh and Milton Diamond, "An Emerging Ethical and Medical Dilemma: Should Physicians Perform Sex Assignment on Infants with Ambiguous Genitalia?," *Michigan Journal of Gender and Law* 7 (2000): 1.

15. Sentencia No. SU-337/99; Sentencia No. T-551/99. These decisions reported in Spanish can be found at http://www.isna.org/node/21. For an English translation of a portion of the decision, see "The Rights of Intersexed Infants and Children: Decision of the Colombian Constitutional Court, Bogotá, Colombia, 12 May 1999 (SU-337/99)," trans. Nohemy Solórzano-Thompson, in *Transgender Rights*, ed. Paisley Currah, Richard M. Juang, and Shannon Price Minter, Minneapolis: University of Minnesota Press, 2006: 122.

16. Milton Diamond and Keith Sigmundson, "Management of Intersexuality: Guidelines for Dealing with Persons with Ambiguous Genitalia," *Archives of Pediatric & Adolescent Medicine* 151 (1997): 1046.

17. John Colapinto, *As Nature Made Him: The Boy Who Was Raised as a Girl*, New York: HarperCollins, 2001.

18. Karkazis, *Fixing Sex*, 256.

19. The major exception is for infants with partial androgen insensitivity syndrome (PAIS). These infants have a Y chromosome and are only partially sensitive to androgens. Eventual gender identity for these infants is not clear, so sex assignment is difficult in these cases.

20. Intersex Society of North America, "Dear ISNA Friends and Supporters," http://www.isna.org/farewell_message.

21. Ibid.

22. Accord Alliance, website homepage, http://www.accordalliance.org/.

23. Karkazis, *Fixing Sex*, 258–259.

24. See, e.g., website of Advocates for Informed Choice, http://aiclegal.org/.

25. Katrina Karkazis and Ellen K. Feder, "Naming the Problem: Disorders and their Meanings," *Lancet* 372 (2008): 2016–2017, http://www.thelancet.com/journals/lancet/article/PIIS0140-6736(08)61858-9/fulltext.

26. For example, males with hypospadias, a condition in which the urethral opening is located somewhere on the shaft of the penis, are often subjected to multiple invasive surgeries to move the opening to the tip of the penis. The harms of these surgeries are similar to the problems suffered by other infants with an intersex condition who have been subjected to surgeries. Therefore, many men who have been treated for hypospadias identify closely with the intersex community, even though hypospadias may not be classified as an intersex condition by some medical experts.

27. Ellen K. Feder and Katrina Karkazis, "What's in a Name? The Controversy over 'Disorders of Sex Development,'" *Hastings Center Report* 38, no. 5 (2008): 33.

28. Emi Koyama, "From 'Intersex' to 'DSD': Toward a Queer Disability Politics of Gender," Intersex Initiative, 2006, http://www.intersexinitiative.org/articles/intersextodsd.html; Intersex Society of North America, "Why Is ISNA Using 'DSD'?," May 24, 2006, http://www.isna.org/node/1066.

29. Milton Diamond and Hazel Glen Beh, "Changes in Management of Children with Differences of Sex," *Nature Clinical Practice: Endocrinology and Metabolism* 4 (2008): 4–5. A working team from Germany, consisting of clinicians, patients, and the patients' families, published ethical recommendations for the treatment of infants born with a DSD; it also supported the use of the term *difference* as opposed to *disorder*. Claudia Wiesemann et al., "Ethical Principles and Recommendations for the Medical Management of Differences of Sex Development (DSD)/Intersex in Children and Adolescents," *European Journal of Pediatrics* 169 (2010): 671–679, http://springerlink.com/content/875242220h6211vu/fulltext.pdf. Advocates for Informed Choice uses both terms, *intersex* and *differences of sex development*: http://www.aiclegal.org/.

30. Elizabeth Reis, "Divergence or Disorder? The Politics of Naming Intersex," *Perspectives in Biology and Medicine* 50 (2007): 535.

31. Julie Butler, "Groom's Intersex Quandary," *West Australian*, Aug. 10, 2002.

32. OII-USA, website homepage, http://www.intersexualite.org/usa.html.

33. OII-USA, "Positions: On a Third Sex," http://www.intersexualite.org/English-Official-Position.html.

34. Alice D. Dreger and April M. Herndon, "Progress and Politics in the Intersex Rights Movement: Feminist Theory in Action," *GLQ: A Journal of Gay and Lesbian Studies* 15 (2009): 208.

35. Karkazis, *Fixing Sex*, 262.

36. Ibid.

NOTES TO CHAPTER 9

1. Alice D. Dreger and April M. Herndon, "Progress and Politics in the Intersex Rights Movement: Feminist Theory in Action," *GLQ: A Journal of Gay and Lesbian Studies* 15 (2009): 199–224.

2. "A Father and Greer Correspond," AIS Support Group website, http://www.medhelp.org/ais/debates/letters/FATHER.HTM.

3. Ibid.

4. Nancy Ehrenreich with Mark Barr, "Intersex Surgery, Female Genital Cutting, and the Selective Condemnation of 'Cultural Practices,'" *Harvard Civil Rights–Civil Liberties Law Review* 40 (2005): 72.

5. "The Girl Child," G.A. Res. 57/189, U.N. Doc. A/RES/57/189 (Feb. 12, 2003), 7th Sess., 2–3.

6. Criminalization of Female Genital Mutilation Act, Pub. L. No. 104-208, § 645, 110 Stat. 3009, 3009-708 (1996) (codified as amended at 18 U.S.C. § 116).

7. See, e.g., Cal. Penal Code § 273.4 (2010); Del. Code § 780 (2010); Florida Statutes § 794.08 (2010); Ga. Code § 16-5-27 (2010); Ill. Code 720 ILCS 5/12-34 (2010).

8. Countries condemning the practice include Canada, the United Kingdom, Sweden, Norway, Denmark, Belgium, Austria, Italy, and Portugal. For a thorough discussion of the laws in these and other countries, see Patricia A. Broussard, "The Importation of Female Genital Mutilation to the West: The Cruelest Cut of All," *University of San Francisco Law Review* 44 (2010): 803–816.

9. Alice D. Dreger, "Ambiguous Sex—or Ambivalent Medicine? Ethical Issues in the Treatment of Intersexuality," *Hastings Center Report* 28 (1998): 28.

10. Cheryl Chase, "'Cultural Practice' or 'Reconstructive Surgery'? U.S. Genital Cutting, the Intersex Movement, and Medical Double Standards," in *Genital Cutting and Transnational Sisterhood: Disputing U.S. Polemics*, ed. Stanlie M. James and Claire C. Robertson, Urbana: University of Illinois Press, 2002: 141.

11. Ibid., 145–146.

12. Ibid.

13. Heino Meyer-Bahlburg, "What Causes Low Rates of Childbearing in Congenital Adrenal Hyperplasia?," *Journal of Clinical Endocrinology and Metabolism* 84 (1999): 1844–1847. For a thorough critique of the use of dexamethasone, see Alice Dreger, Ellen K Feder, and Anne Tamar-Mattis, "Preventing Homosexuality (and Uppity Women) in the Womb?," *Bioethics Forum* (blog), Hastings Center, June 29, 2010, http://www.thehastings-center.org/Bioethicsforum/Post.aspx?id=4754&blogid=140.

14. Ki Namaste, "Tragic Misreading: Queer Theory's Erasure of Transgender Subjectivity," in *Queer Studies: A Lesbian, Gay, Bisexual, and Transgender Anthology*, ed. Brett Beemyn and Mickey Eliason, New York: NYU Press, 1996: 197. Legal authorities often duplicate this medical approach. Just as the medical community is uncomfortable with infant genitalia and bodies that do not fit a male/female norm, many legal tribunals require transsexuals to undergo a "complete" medical transition, including genital surgery, before they will allow an amendment to their official records. In other words, the law often does not recognize people who do not fit into clear binary sex categories.

15. Sharon E. Preves, "Out of the O.R. and into the Streets: Exploring the Impact of Intersex Media Activism," *Research in Political Sociology* 13 (2004): 179.

16. Raven Kaldera, "Dangerous Intersections: Intersex and Transgender Differences," http://ravenkaldera.org/intersection/DangerousIntersections.html.

17. Emi Koyama, "From 'Intersex' to 'DSD': Toward a Queer Disability Politics of Gender," Intersex Initiatives, 2006, http://www.intersexinitiative.org/articles/intersextodsd.html.

18. Ibid.

19. Heather Cassell, "California Looms as Marriage Equality Battleground," *Bay Area Reporter*, July 5, 2007, http://www.ebar.com/news/article.php?sec=news&article=1972.

20. Emi Koyama, "Adding the 'I': Does Intersex Belong in the LGBT Movement?," Intersex Initiatives, http://www.intersexinitiative.org/articles/lgbti.html.

21. Karla Jay, *Tales of the Lavender Menace: A Memoir of Liberation*, New York: Basic Books, 2000: 137–138; Lillian Faderman, *Odd Girls and Twilight Lovers*, New York: Columbia University Press, 1991: 212.

22. Anna Kirkland, "Victorious Transsexuals in the Courtroom: A Challenge for Feminist Legal Theory," *Law and Social Inquiry* 28 (2003): 1.

23. Shannon Minter, "Do Transsexuals Dream of Gay Rights?," in *Transgender Rights*, ed. Paisley Currah, Richard M. Juang, and Shannon Price Minter, Minneapolis: University of Minnesota Press, 2006: 155.

24. See Nan Alamilla Boyd, "Bodies in Motion: Lesbian and Transsexual Histories," in *A Queer World: The Center for Lesbian and Gay Studies Reader*, ed. Martin Duberman, New York: NYU Press, 1997: 143–145.

25. Nancy J. Knauer, "Gender Matters: Making the Case for Trans Inclusion," *Pierce Law Review* 6 (2007): 3.

26. Minter, "Do Transsexuals Dream of Gay Rights?," 142.

27. Ibid.

28. For an excellent analysis of the development of the gay movement and its change in focus, see ibid.

29. On April 6, 2011, Representative Barney Frank introduced a gender identity inclusive ENDA in the House of Representatives. Chris Johnson, "ENDA Makes Debut in 112th Congress," *Washington Blade*, April 6, 2011, http://www.washingtonblade.com/2011/04/06/enda-makes-debut-in-112th-congress/. The Senate introduced a similar bill on April 23, 2011. Steve Rothaus, "HRC: Inclusive Employment Non-Discrimination Act (ENDA) Introduced in U.S. Senate," *Miami Herald*, April 14, 2011, http://miamiherald.typepad.com/gaysouthflorida/2011/04/hrc-inclusive-employment-non-discrimination-act-enda-introduced-in-us-senate.html.

NOTES TO CHAPTER 10

1. Sentencia No. SU-337/99; Sentencia No. T-551/99. These decisions reported in Spanish can be found at http://www.isna.org/node/21. For an English translation of a portion of Sentencia SU-337/99, see "The Rights of Intersexed Infants and Children: Decision of the Colombian Constitutional Court, Bogotá, Colombia, 12 May 1999 (SU-337/99)," trans. Nohemy Solórzano-Thompson, in *Transgender Rights*, ed. Paisley Currah, Richard M. Juang, and Shannon Price Minter, Minneapolis: University of Minnesota Press, 2006: 122–138. For a more thorough discussion of this issue, see chapter 2.

2. In re A, 16 FLR 715 (Family Court of Australia 1993).

3. "Gender Warrior Wins Case against Surgeon," *Deutsche Welle*, June 2, 2008, http://www.dw-world.de/dw/article/0,2144,3111505,00.html.

4. In re Marriage of C and D (falsely called C), 35 FLR 340 (1979); W v. W, Fam. 111, 58 BMLR 15 (Fam. 111 2001).

5. Wood v. C.G. Studios, 660 F. Supp. 176 (E.D. Pa. 1987).

6. DiMarco v. Wyoming Dep't of Corrections, 2007 WL 172189 (Wyo. 2007); Tucker v. Evans, 2009 WL 799175 (E.D. Mich. 2009).

7. The Colombia lawsuit was initiated because doctors told parents that they would not proceed without a court order.

8. Anne Tamar-Mattis, executive director of Advocates for Informed Choice, personal interview, Aug. 30, 2010.

9. Ibid.

10. U.S. Department of State, "7 Fam 1350 Appendix M: Gender Change," *Foreign Affairs Manual*, vol. 7, http://www.state.gov/documents/organization/143160.pdf.

11. Ibid.

12. Tamar-Mattis interview.

13. Chapter 2 contains a detailed discussion of these arguments.

14. Human Rights Commission of the City of San Francisco, "A Human Rights Investigation into the Medical 'Normalization' of Intersex People: A Report of a Hearing of the San Francisco Human Rights Commission," Apr. 28, 2005: 17–18, http://www.sf-hrc.org/ftp/uploadedfiles/sfhumanrights/Committee_Meetings/Lesbian_Gay_Bisexual_Transgender/SFHRC%20Intersex%20Report(1).pdf.

15. Ibid.

16. For a general discussion of international human rights protections, see Office of the United Nations High Commissioner for Human Rights, "International Human Rights Law," http://www.ohchr.org/en/professionalinterest/Pages/InternationalLaw.aspx.

17. Office of the United Nations High Commissioner for Human Rights, "Convention on the Rights of the Child," Nov. 20, 1989, http://www2.ohchr.org/english/law/crc.htm.

18. Skinner v. Oklahoma, 316 U.S. 535 (1942).

19. Susan Jones, "Obama Directs U.S. to Sign First New Human Rights Treaty of the 21st Century," CNSNews.com, July 27, 2009, http://www.cnsnews.com/news/article/51614.

20. United Nations, "Convention on the Rights of Persons with Disabilities," Dec. 13, 2006, http://www.un.org/disabilities/default.asp?id=150.

21. Americans with Disabilities Act, 42 U.S.C. § 12101 et seq. (1990).

22. Ibid., §§ 12132, 12182.

23. Ibid., § 12102(1).

24. Ibid., § 12102(2)(b).

25. Many of these surgeries have caused incontinence and other urinary tract problems, as well as pain and other problems while engaging in sex. Some adults who were subjected to these surgeries in their childhood assert that it is the surgery itself that has destroyed their ability to engage in satisfactory sex and has impaired a major life function.

26. Americans with Disabilities Act, 42 U.S.C. § 12102(2)(b).

27. Ibid., § 12102(3).

28. U.S. Equal Employment Opportunity Commission, "Section 902 Definition of the Term Disability: 902.8(d) Regarded as Having a Substantially Limiting Impairment," http://www.eeoc.gov/policy/docs/902cm.html#902.8d.

29. One woman with XY chromosomes who sought to adopt a child was refused the right to adopt by an agency because of her intersex condition.

30. Issues have arisen in school sports about whether a child with an intersex condition should participate on the girls' or boys' athletic teams. As more children with an intersex condition are not surgically altered, issues relating to bathroom and locker room use will likely arise.

31. David R. Carson and Deborah A. Dorfman, "Investigative Report Regarding the 'Ashley Treatment,'" Washington Protection and Advocacy System, May 8, 2007, http://www.disabilityrightswa.org/home/Full_Report_InvestigativeReportRegardingtheAshley-Treatment.pdf. The WPAS is now named Disability Rights Washington.

32. Ashley X did not have an intersex condition; she was born with profound developmental disabilities. The reasoning that the WPAS applied to a child with developmental disabilities would apply with equal force to a child born with an intersex condition.

33. Daniel F. Gunther and Douglas S. Diekema, "Attenuating Growth in Children with Profound Developmental Disability: A New Approach to an Old Dilemma" *Archives of Pediatric and Adolescent Medicine* 160 (2006): 1014, http://archpedi.ama-assn.org/cgi/content/full/160/10/1013.

34. Ibid.

35. Dave Reynolds, "Advocates Speak Out and Call for Investigations over 'Ashley Treatment,'" *Inclusion Daily Express*, Jan. 12, 2007, http://www.inclusiondaily.com/archives/07/01/12/011207waashleyx.htm; William Peace, "The Ashley Treatment and the Making of a Pillow Angel," *Counterpunch*, Jan. 18, 2007, http://www.counterpunch.org/peace01182007.html.

36. Carson and Dorfman, "Investigative Report Regarding the 'Ashley Treatment.'"

37. Ibid.

38. Ibid.

39. Recommending external review of these procedures does not imply that when parents approve either treatments similar to the Ashley treatment for profoundly disabled children or genital surgery for infants with an intersex condition that they are motivated by anything other than love and the best interests of their children. These procedures are different from other life altering decisions that parents make for their children because of the limited information available about the benefits and risks and the difficulty separating the parents' and the child's best interests. For an excellent discussion of the pros and cons of various approaches when the issue involves growth attenuation of profoundly disabled children, see Benjamin S. Wilfond et al., "Navigating Growth Attenuation in Children with Profound Disabilities: Children's Interests, Family Decision-Making and Community Concerns," *Hastings Center Report*, Nov.–Dec. 2010: 27.

40. See online comments to "Leading Article: Consensus Statement on Management of Intersex Disorders," *Archives of Disease in Childhood*, http://adc.bmj.com/content/91/7/554/reply. A recent report from a German working group addressing the bioethical concerns rejects use of the term *disorder* and instead uses *difference*. Claudia Wiesemann et al., "Ethical Principles and Recommendations for the Medical Management of Differences of Sex Development (DSD)/Intersex in Children and Adolescents," *European Journal of Pediatrics* 169 (2010): 671–679, http://springerlink.com/content/87524222oh6211vu/fulltext.pdf.

41. Curtis E. Hinkle, "Why Is OII Not Using the Term DSD or 'Disorders of Sexual Development'?," Intersexualite.org, http://www.intersexualite.org/Response_to_Intersex_Initiative.html.

42. Dianne Pothier and Richard Devlin, *Critical Disability Theory: Essays in Philosophy, Politics, and Law*, Vancouver: UBC Press, 2006; Nancy Ehrenreich with Mark Barr, "Intersex Surgery, Female Genital Cutting, and the Selective Condemnation of 'Cultural Practices,'" *Harvard Civil Rights–Civil Liberties Law Review* 40 (2005): 71; Jennifer L. Levi and Bennett H. Klein, "Pursuing Protection for Transgender People through Disability Laws," in *Transgender Rights*, ed. Paisley Currah, Richard M. Juang, and Shannon Price Minter, Minneapolis: University of Minnesota Press, 2006: 74–89.

43. Esther Morris, "The Missing Vagina Monologue and Beyond," *Sojourner Women's Health Edition*, October 2000, http://mrkh.org/files/The_Missing_Vagina_Monologue_and_Beyond.pdf.

44. See, e.g., 20 U.S.C. § 1681 et seq., Title IX of the Education Amendments of 1972, prohibiting sex discrimination in education; 42 U.S.C.A. § 2000e et seq., Title VII of the Civil Rights Act of 1964, forbidding sex discrimination in employment; and the Patient Protection and Affordable Care Act, Pub. L. No. 111-148, 124 Stat. 119–124 Stat. 1025 (Mar. 23, 2010), prohibiting discrimination in the provision of health care services.

45. See Joan C. Williams and Nancy Segal, "Beyond the Maternal Wall: Relief for Family Caregivers Who Are Discriminated Against on the Job," *Harvard Women's Law Journal* 26 (2003): 77 (citing Chi v. Age Group, Ltd., 1996 WL 627580, at *2 (S.D.N.Y. 1996)); Martinez v. NBC, 49 F. Supp. 2d 305, 309–311 (S.D.N.Y. 1999); Fuller v. GTE Corp., 926 F. Supp. 653, 656 (M.D. Tenn. 1996); Bass v. Chem. Banking Corp., 1996 WL 374151, at *1 (S.D.N.Y. July 2, 1996); Piantanida v. Wyman Center, Inc., 927 F. Supp. 1226 (E.D. Mo. 1996).

46. Gedulig v. Aiello, 417 U.S. 484 (1974); General Electric Co. v. Gilbert, 429 U.S. 125 (1976).

47. See, e.g., Williamson v. A. G. Edwards & Sons, Inc., 876 F.2d 69, 70 (8th Cir. 1989); DeSantis v. Pacific Tel. & Tel. Co., 608 F.2d 327, 330–331 (9th Cir. 1979). This approach has been followed in a number of later cases including *Simonton v. Runyon*, 232 F.3d 33, 36–37 (2d Cir. 2000); *Spearman v. Ford Motor Co.*, 231 F.3d 1080, 1085–1086 (7th Cir. 2000); and *Higgins v. New Balance Athletic Shoe, Inc.*, 194 F.3d 252, 261 (1st Cir. 1999).

48. See, e.g., Holloway v. Arthur Anderson and Co., 566 F.2d 659, 663–664 (9th Cir. 1977); Sommers v. Budget Marketing, Inc., 667 F.2d 748, 750 (8th Cir. 1982); Voyles v. Ralph K. Davies Med. Ctr., 403 F. Supp. 456, 457 (N.D. Cal. 1975), aff'd mem., 570 F.2d 354 (9th Cir. 1978); Powell v. Read's, Inc., 436 F. Supp. 369, 370–371 (D. Md. 1977); Grossman v. Bernards Township Bd. of Educ., 1975 WL 302, at *1 (D.N.J. Sept. 10, 1975); Dobre v. Nat'l R.R. Passenger Corp., 850 F. Supp. 284, 285–286 (E.D. Pa. 1993); Doe v. U.S. Postal Serv., 1985 WL 9446, at *1 (D.D.C. June 12, 1985); Terry v. EEOC, 1980 WL 334, at *1 (E.D. Wis. Dec. 10, 1980).

49. Wood v. C.G. Studios, 660 F. Supp. 176 (E.D. Pa. 1987).

50. Price Waterhouse v. Hopkins, 490 U.S. 228 (1989).

51. Ibid., 235.

52. Ibid.

53. See, e.g., Back v. Hastings on Hudson Union Free Sch. Dist., 365 F.3d 107, 120 (2d Cir. 2004); Santiago-Ramos v. Centennial P.R. Wireless Corp., 217 F.3d 46, 57 (1st Cir. 2000); Sheehan v. Donlen Corp., 173 F.3d 1039, 1044–1045 (7th Cir. 1999) (holding that mothers who suffered discrimination because of their employers' assumptions about their ability to be both mothers and good workers constitutes impermissible sex stereotyping).

54. Back v. Hastings on Hudson Union Free Sch. Dist., 365 F.3d 107, 120 (2d Cir. 2004).

55. Knussman v. Maryland, 272 F.3d 625 (4th Cir. 2001).

56. Ibid., 636.

57. See, e.g., Rene v. MGM Grand Hotel, Inc., 305 F.3d 1061, 1069 (9th Cir. 2002), cert. denied, 538 U.S. 922 (2003); Nichols v. Azteca Rest. Enters., Inc., 256 F. 3d 864 (9th Cir. 2001); Schmedding v. Tnemec Co., Inc., 187 F.3d 862 (8th Cir. 1999). A number of courts continue to deny recovery to gays and lesbians if they allege they were harassed because of their sexual orientation. See, e.g., Dandan v. Radisson Hotel Lisle, 2000 WL 336528 (N.D. Ill. 2000); Mims v. Carrier Corp., 88 F. Supp. 2d 706, 714 (E.D. Tex. 2000); Higgins v. New Balance, 194 F.3d 252, 259 (1st Cir. 1999); Hamner v. St. Vincent Hospital and Health Care Center, Inc., 224 F.3d 701, 704 (7th Cir. 2000).

58. Rene v. MGM Grand Hotel, Inc., 305 F.3d 1061, 1069 (9th Cir. 2002), cert. denied, 538 U.S. 922 (2003).

59. See, e.g., Smith v. City of Salem, 378 F.3d 566, 575 (6th Cir. 2004); Barnes v. Cincinnati, 410 F.3d 729 (6th Cir. 2005); Rosa v. Park West Bank & Trust, 214 F.3d 213 (1st Cir. 2000); and Schwenk v. Hartford, 204 F.3d 1187 (9th Cir. 2000). The sex stereotyping theory has not been universally accepted in all cases involving transsexuals. See, e.g., Etsitty v. Utah Transit Authority, 502 F.3d 1215 (10th Cir. 2007).

60. Smith v. City of Salem, 378 F.3d 566, 575 (6th Cir. 2004).

61. Schroer v. Billington, 557 F. Supp. 2d 293 (D.C.C. 2008).

62. Ibid., 305.

63. Ibid., 306.

64. Ibid., 306–307.

65. Wood v. C.G. Studios, 660 F. Supp. 176 (E.D. Pa. 1987).

66. The Patient Protection and Affordable Care Act, Pub. L. No. 111-148, 124 Stat. 119–124 Stat. 1025 (Mar. 23, 2010).

67. Before enactment of this legislation, gender discrimination in the health care industry was rampant. Some women were denied insurance coverage on the basis of their having a "preexisting condition" if they had undergone a Caesarean section or were the victims of domestic abuse. Other women were charged higher rates than men were charged, from 4 to 48 percent higher, on the rationale that women incur higher health care costs than men do. In some cases, women who did not smoke were charged higher premiums than male smokers were charged. Denise Grady, "Overhaul Will Lower the Costs of Being a Woman," New York Times, Mar. 29, 2010, http://www.nytimes.com/2010/03/30/health/30women.html.

68. The Patient Protection and Affordable Care Act, 42 U.S.C. § 18116(a) (2010).

69. National Gay and Lesbian Task Force, "State Nondiscrimination Laws in the U.S.," last updated July 1, 2009, http://www.thetaskforce.org/downloads/reports/issue_maps/non_discrimination_7_09_color.pdf.

70. Ibid.

71. See Employment Nondiscrimination Act of 2009, S. 1584, 111th Cong. (2009); Employment Nondiscrimination Act of 2007, H.R. 3685, 110th Cong. (2007); Employment Nondiscrimination Act of 2003, S. 1705, 108th Cong. (2003); Employment Nondiscrimination Act of 2001, S. 1284, 107th Cong. (2001); Employment Nondiscrimination Act of 1999, S. 1276, 106th Cong. (1999); Employment Nondiscrimination Act of 1997, S. 869, 105th Cong. (1997); Employment Nondiscrimination Act of 1996, S. 2056, 104th Cong. (1996); Employment Nondiscrimination Act of 1995, H.R. 1863, 104th Cong. (1995); Employment Nondiscrimination Act of 1994, H.R. 4636, 103rd Cong. (1994).

NOTES TO THE CONCLUSION

1. Katrina Karkazis, Fixing Sex: Intersex, Medical Authority, and Lived Experience, Durham: Duke University Press, 2008: 134–135; Anne Tamar-Mattis, "XXY Offers a New View of Life in an Intersex Body," Berkeley Journal of Gender, Law, and Justice 24 (2009): 70–71.

2. Mary Bernstein, Anna-Maria Marshall, and Scott Barclay, "The Challenge of Law: Sexual Orientation, Gender Identity, and Social Movements," in Queer Mobilizations, ed. Scott Barclay, Mary Bernstein, and Anna-Maria Marshall, New York: NYU Press, 2009: 1.

3. Wood v. C.G. Studios, 660 F. Supp. 176 (E.D. Pa. 1987).

4. Nancy Ehrenreich, "Subordination and Symbiosis: Mechanisms of Mutual Support between Subordinating Systems," UMKC Law Review 71 (2002): 251.

5. Ibid. (maintaining that the elimination of a subordinating system requires an attack on the "entire edifice of interlocking oppressions"); Victor C. Romero, "Rethinking Minority Coalition Building: Valuing Self-Sacrifice, Stewardship and Anti-subordination," Villanova Law Review 50 (2005): 823 (explaining that the focus on self-interest makes minority coalition building difficult to create and sustain); Francisco Valdes, "Sex and Race in Queer Legal Culture: Ruminations on Identities and Interconnectivities," Southern California Review of Law and Women's Studies 5 (1995): 25 (calling for interconnectivity as a strategy); Darren Hutchinson, "Ignoring the Sexualization of Race: Heteronormativity,

Critical Race Theory, and Anti-racist Politics," *Buffalo Law Review* 47 (1999): 1 (discussing the failure of antiracist scholarship to address the relationship between racial oppression and other forms of subordination); Richard Delgado, "Linking Arms: Recent Books on Interracial Coalitions as an Avenue of Social Reform," *Cornell Law Review* 88 (2003): 855 (explaining how the goal of assimilation has contributed to minority coalition problems).

6. Samuel A. Marcosson, "Multiplicities of Subordination: The Challenge of Real Inter-group Conflicts of Interest," *UMKC Law Review* 71 (2002): 459; Robert S. Chang and Jerome McCristal Culp, Jr., "After Intersectionality," *UMKC Law Review* 71 (2002): 485.

7. Joan C. Williams, "Fretting in the Force Fields: Why the Distribution of Social Power Has Proved So Hard to Change," *UMKC Law Review* 71 (2002): 500–501.

8. Jill M. Bystydzienski and Steven P. Schacht, introduction to *Forging Radical Alliance across Difference: Coalition Politics for the New Millennium*, ed. Jill M. Bystydzienski and Steven P. Schacht, Lanham, MD: Rowman and Littlefield, 2001: 6.

9. See ibid. (analyzing social justice movements and providing detailed analysis of some radical alliances that were ineffective and short-lived as well as projects that have been successful in bringing about meaningful change).

10. Sharon E. Preves, *Intersex and Identity: The Contested Self*, New Brunswick: Rutgers University Press, 2003: 148.

11. See cases discussed in chapter 4.

12. See cases discussed in chapter 5.

13. See cases discussed in chapter 6.

# Index

# About the Author

JULIE A. GREENBERG is Professor of Law and former Associate Dean at Thomas Jefferson School of Law.